DRINKS,
DRUGS, AND
DO-GOODERS

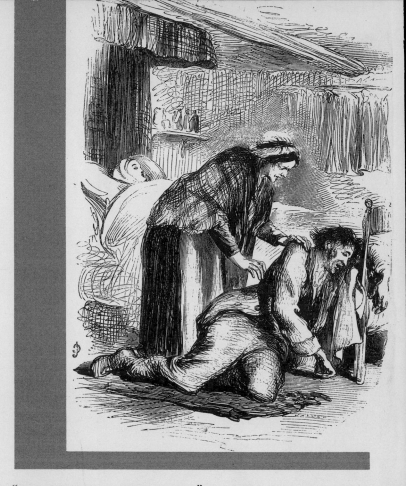

"THE DRUNKARD RETURNS HOME"
"THE DRUNKARD'S PROMISE"
TYPICAL MESSAGE FROM THE TEMPERANCE MOVEMENT
IN 1867

THE FREE PRESS, New York
COLLIER-MACMILLAN PUBLISHERS, London

DRINKS, DRUGS, AND DO-GOODERS

Charles E. Goshen

Library of Congress Cataloging in Publication Data

Goshen, Charles E
    Drinks, drugs, and do-gooders.

    1. Liquor problem—United States. 2. Drug abuse—
United States. 3. Drug abuse—Treatment—United States.
I. Title.
HV5292.G63   362.2'9'0973   72–93309
    ISBN 0–02–912620–7

The Free Press
A Division of Macmillan Publishing Co., Inc.

Collier-Macmillan Canada Ltd.

printing number

1 2 3 4 5 6 7 8 9 10

In appreciation of the considerable help they have given, this book is dedicated to:

PAT

BOB AND MARTITA

ANNE AND BRUCE

JOE AND BETTY

MIKIE AND MILDRED

and to many medical and nursing students of Vanderbilt University who constituted the first audience for most of these remarks

CONTENTS

PREFACE

THE social problems related to drugs and alcohol have excited widespread interest and alarm, and have mobilized massive government anti-drug programs. A wide variety of viewpoints colors a diverse array of writings on the subject, perhaps adding more confusion than clarification to the issues. This book discusses the subject from a viewpoint which seeks practical solutions, hopefully devoid of the mythology which typifies current programs.

The author writes from the vantage point of a psychiatrist and a professor of management, who has studied drug and alcohol cases in respect to their problems of social adjustment. A historical perspective is developed in order to draw a picture of the cultural setting in which the current problem exists. Few efforts in the past have demonstrated, as this book does, the extensive common denominators which can be found between the past and the present. In many ways, history is now repeating itself, and repeating past failures, not successes. The lessons of the past have not been learned. Current drug and alcohol problems might well turn out to be insolvable, but any disappointment we experience on this score should prompt us to focus our efforts on the prevention of new problems of the future.

THE AUTHOR

DRINKS, DRUGS, AND DO-GOODERS

INTRODUCTION

THE United States has led the world in the steps ensuring and protecting the rights of individuals. Each period of our history has seen landmark decisions and practices put into effect that extend the right of the individual to live his own life relatively free from the constraints of society. Nevertheless, we have also led the world in fruitless experiments to control people's moral behavior. As civilization progresses and develops broader and more tolerant viewpoints toward old moralistic restraints, we increase, rather than decrease, our efforts to impose various prohibitions on people whose behavior happens to suffer the disapproval of the ill-organized but powerful, self-appointed custodians of our morality.

The "Noble Experiment" of National Prohibition brought about by the Eighteenth Amendment and repealed by the Twenty-first was only one of many similar attempts to achieve what should now be apparent as the impossible— to restrain people from finding pleasure in what some other groups of people condemn. We are currently facing, in the 1970s, major social dislocations, and alarms caused by the spread of drug abuse. We are facing the problem in much the same way we dealt with the alcohol problem in the 1920s, and with strikingly similar results.

We have long recognized that the kind of people who chose to make their homes in the United States were prepared to exert great efforts, endure great hazards, and show great persistence in resisting political tyranny. Americans have long sought opportunities for upgrading their lots in life and have always championed the underdog and defied those who would acquire excessive power over others. Somehow, however, our country has failed to recognize something equally obvious. This is the fact that no set of forces or circumstances brings forth as much ingenuity, patience, and resourcefulness in Americans as does the pursuit of personal pleasure. The fact that there also exists a puritanical tradition that regards pleasure as something evil and wasteful was always evident on the American scene, but more for its preachments than its practices, even in the early New England colonial days when it was first introduced. Each generation nostalgically looks back to some earlier time in history when people allegedly behaved the way those preachments demanded, but rarely did such practices prevail. Riots and violence have always been with us, sex—licit or otherwise—was never stamped out, and Americans have always managed to consume more than their fair share of alcohol. Gambling was more than a game in the past; it was literally a way of life, a way of doing business that produced our industrialized economy.

The current issue of drug abuse is essentially indistinguishable from the problem of alcohol. The only significant difference is the fact that the drug problem is insignificant in size when compared with the alcohol problem. Otherwise, the differences are merely a matter of taste—in the same way that some alcoholics drink too much beer and others consume too much Scotch. Equating the two sets of problems in no way diminishes their importance, but it will serve to rid the present system of many of the inconsistencies that impede rational solutions.

THE PLEDGE

"I promise not to buy, sell or give
Alcoholic liquors while I live;
From all tobacco I'll abstain
And never take God's name in vain."

Composed by Frances Willard, early leader of the Women's Christian Temperance Union. "Taking the pledge" was the symbol of commitment to the temperance cause.

We Americans specifically need to face the facts of drug and alcohol abuse with the following set of conditions: (1) solutions to the problems must concentrate on programs that can reduce the number and severity of the cases; (2) other people's personal preferences, likes and dislikes, and personal crusades concerning solutions must be set aside. This means that, in order to be effective, programs might well entail the establishment of practices that many people do not like or want. For instance, if legalization of marihuana can bring the abuse of this drug under better control than it is now, then it is worth trying. The fact that many people might not want it this way should have no bearing on the decision. Unfortunately, our present system of control has been designed solely in accordance with certain people's special preferences, and without regard to the necessity of finding solutions that work.

In any event, this book is meant to be a contribution to this viewpoint—a survey of the over-all cost and over-all effectiveness of our current system of control. Some suggestions are offered, far short of a comprehensive program, for solutions.

Chapter

1

THE GROWTH OF A PROHIBITION MOVEMENT

THE EARLY YEARS

APPARENTLY, the first effort in the American colonies to control the use of alcoholic beverages was made in the Colony of Georgia in 1733. The experiment established a model of citizen defiance of the law that should have, but did not, become a warning to subsequent planners. The Trustees of the Colony (in England) decided that rum was an evil that should be kept out of the Colony, so they ordered Governor George Oglethorpe to prohibit its importation or manufacture. The neighboring colonists in South Carolina apparently saw the prohibition in Georgia as a great potential source of revenue, so there almost immediately developed a flourishing smuggling trade in rum, chiefly through the coastal ports. The model thus set became a standard one, repeated many times afterwards—namely, the recognition by entrepreneurs that prohibition opens the door to profitable business opportunities. Many people were ready to take advantage of these opportunities. In addition to the rumrunning, a network of salesmen sprang up to distribute the liquor to every corner of the Colony, illegal barrooms were set up in homes and in the backs of stores, and local producers began to learn the art of distillation. It became clear that the colonists did not regard these violations of the law as immoral acts. The early offenders arrested were brought to trial before juries of their peers, in line with their rights as Englishmen, so few, if any, convictions were handed down. Before the law was finally repealed, other convenient precedents were established that forecast future responses when other experiments were tried. For example, public officials became involved in sharing profits from the illegal sale of rum.

The Continental Congress in February, 1777, passed a resolution requesting the state legislatures to pass laws prohibiting the use of corn and wheat by distillers, apparently to conserve grain supplies for bread rather than to suppress the consumption of whiskey. More important, perhaps, the resolution indicated that American corn whiskey was already becoming so widely manufactured and consumed that it was attracting notice as a major product. At the time, the most popular distilled liquor was rum, imported from the West Indies, or manufactured from molasses imported from that region. However, rum was available only in and near coastal seaports. The grain-growing farmers farther west, and especially those west of the Appalachians, discovered that it was much more profitable to convert their grains to whiskey than to ship raw grains to market, because of the difficulties in moving heavy cargoes over the poor roads of the times. Pittsburgh, then Kentucky, became main centers for converting grain to whiskey. Although the resolution of the Continental Congress produced no response, its underlying sentiments were

RESOLUTION OF THE CONTINENTAL CONGRESS, FEBRUARY, 1784

Resolved, That it be recommended to the several legislatures of the United States immediately to pass laws the most effectual for putting an immediate stop to the pernicious practice of distilling grain, by which the most extensive evils are likely to be derived, if not quickly prevented.

expressed later in the first Revenue Act of the new constitutional government.

Alexander Hamilton, the first Secretary of the Treasury, proposed that revenue for the new federal government be raised by a general tax on all imports and by an internal tax on snuff, carriages, legal documents, and spirits. These proposals were strongly opposed in Congress, but passed, nevertheless, as the Revenue Act of 1791. Efforts to collect the tax led to the Whiskey Rebellion among the distillers of western Pennsylvania in 1794. President Washington sent the federal militia to suppress the uprising, thus surviving the first challenge to the authority of the new federal government. At the time, whiskey was selling for only about twenty-five cents per gallon, and the tax was seven cents. For most of the next hundred years, the federal government's revenues were made up almost entirely of the liquor tax, sale of public lands, and import duties.

Thomas Jefferson was opposed to the system of excise taxes, and fulfilled his party's pledge by having the law repealed in 1802. During the War of 1812 the law was reinstated because of the decline in revenues from import duties. The tax on whiskey was increased in 1814, but in

1817 the law was again repealed. It was not until the outbreak of the Civil War that a liquor tax was again levied, as a wartime measure, and it has been continuously in effect since then. The Act of 1862 imposed a tax of twenty cents a gallon. The following table shows the amount of revenue collected from liquor taxes since that time:

1868	$ 6,805,000
1875	61,226,000
1900	183,420,000
1925 (Prohibition)	25,905,000
1950	2,219,202,000
1966	3,814,000,000
1970	4,746,000,000

EARLY ANTI-DRINKING LAWS

1620: Governor Winthrop of Massachusetts banned the drinking of toasts.

1642: Maryland levied a fine of 100 pounds of tobacco for public drunkenness.

1650: Connecticut limited tippling to one-half hour per sitting.

1658: Maryland provided for punishment of public drunks in stocks.

1668: New Jersey banned drinking after 9:00 P.M.

1697: New York ordered saloons closed on Sundays.

1719: New Hampshire made it illegal to sell liquor to someone already under the influence.

THE TEMPERANCE MOVEMENT

The first temperance organization, The Union Temperance Society, was, apparently, founded by a physician, Dr. Billy Clark, in Saratoga, New York, in 1808. It did not last long, nor did it spread. However, during the 1820s other temperance societies appeared rather rapidly in Connecticut, Massachusetts, New York, Rhode Island, Vermont, New Hampshire, and Pennsylvania. The southern states were conspicuously uninvolved in the early stages of the movement, perhaps because of their familiarity with the failure of the Georgia experiment with prohibition. Legal prohibition, however, was not a universal cause advocated by all the temperance leaders. Many of them more realistically saw that only through public education could inroads be made into the excessive drinking habits of some elements in the population. The early, active organization of a strong temperance movement would seem to indicate that there was widespread awareness of the evils of drinking. A theme running through most of the movement was that the evils of alcohol particularly affected the working class, coupled with the assumption that upper-class citizens could be trusted to use alcohol with more restraint.

Another cultural factor that tended to add an aura of sin to drinking, particularly as it applied to the working class, was the custom of orienting drinking habits to the neighborhood saloon where workingmen found access to masculine society and where other practices, including gambling and prostitution, took place, which women in particular frowned upon. The pattern of the saloon as the "workman's private club," comparable to the English Pub, was finally abolished during Prohibition, to be replaced by drinking patterns that included women. In any event, during the nineteenth century, the temperance movement, spearheaded by the Anti-Saloon League, leveled its attack largely against the saloon for the many evils it supposedly embodied, not the least being its exclusion of women (respectable women, that is).

In 1836, the American Temperance Union claimed to be a national organization with more than 8,000 local branches

GERMANS AND BEER

"We have had great changes in our population. During the 35 years ending December 31, 1881, 9,858,205 immigrants landed on our shores, of whom 3,052,881 came from Germany. Nearly 5,000,000 people in the U.S. were either German-born or German in the second degree. The infusion into our population of so many Germans, and their natural increase, with their social customs and strong national predilections, particularly their national devotion to malt liquors through so many centuries, and their settling in large numbers in our cities and other localities, and maintaining the habits and ideas of the father-land, have produced, as might naturally be expected, a deep impression upon American society. Lager beer has come into a prominence never dreamed of prior to 1850, and everywhere conspicuously challenges attention. In 1850, only 36,000,000 gallons of malt liquors were consumed in the U.S., or one and two fifths gallons per capita. In the year ending May 1, 1883, 537,-000,000 gallons, or ten gallons per capita were consumed."

From Dr. Daniel Dorchester, The Liquor Problem in All Ages, *1884.*

and 1,500,000 members. It was launched largely by lay-men, but extensively supported by various Protestant sects. In the 1840s, the movement began to enlist support among medical societies, and one after another of these medical groups passed resolutions pledging their members to avoid prescribing alcohol for their patients. There is little evidence, however, that these resolutions were extensively honored. Instead, the passing of resolutions that were then ignored became common practice in many circles. Public denunciations of the evils of alcohol were easily evoked, but they seemed universally to indicate the kind of behavior expected of others, not what was intended for oneself.

By the 1840s temperance lobbies became active in some of the state legislatures, chiefly to secure legislation to restrict the numbers and locations of saloons. In New York, a local option law was passed providing for local restrictions where the citizens demanded them. With the exception of New York City, 728 out of 856 towns in the state passed ordinances prohibiting the opening of any more saloons. Interestingly, the existing saloons supported this legislation, because it limited competition. This practice was representative of others to follow, in which bootleggers teamed up with prohibitionists to maintain the restrictive laws that provided them with a profitable business. In 1844, the legislature of the new state of Oregon passed a law forbidding the sale of "ardent spirits"—an event regarded as a great temperance victory by its proponents. There still had not developed any organized opposition to the movement, and none did develop until some time after the Civil War.

A great deal of attention came to be focused on the state of Maine as a target for the movement. At the time, Maine was considered by many Americans as a model-setting state that tended to influence what happened elsewhere.

State-wide prohibition became a goal, and the first step
toward achieving it was reached in 1843 when the city of
Portland passed an ordinance that stopped the licensing
of grog shops. In 1844, a bill was introduced in the state
legislature, passed by the House, but defeated in the Senate. Petitions from thousands of voters were collected the
next year, and a Bill managed to pass both houses of the
legislature in 1846. The law set a limit on the amount of
liquor that could be sold by wholesalers and importers and
permitted local towns to set limits on the licensing of saloons. These provisions did not satisfy the supporters of
the temperance movement, and stricter laws were lobbied
for until 1851 when one was passed that prohibited the
sale and manufacture of intoxicating liquors. Heavy fines
were provided for violators. The grog shops were given
two months to close down, after which an active enforcement campaign got underway, and rumrunning from Canada became a major industry. It is interesting that John
Stuart Mill, the British economist, wrote an essay at the
time predicting the failure of the Maine prohibition experiment.

During the Civil War, the government's need for revenue led to a substantial increase in the alcohol tax. It
advanced from twenty cents per gallon in 1862 to $2 per
gallon by 1868. The popularity of the temperance movement and the absence, until then, of organized opposition
left the government in a position where it believed it could
"tax alcohol to death" with impunity. The confiscatory level
of the tax at the end of the war drove many distillers and
wholesalers out of business, which seemed to displease few
people who were then vocal about such matters. However,
a new element entered the picture, which altered the government's policies. The high tax made it very profitable for
those doing business in liquors who could avoid paying

WHAT THE GIN-SHOP DOES.

This is the *Woman*, with woe-begone face,
The wife of the drunkard, in rags and disgrace,
Who is served by the lady, all jewels and lace,
The wife of the landlord who coins his bright gold
Out of the ruin of youthful and old,
Who drink the strong liquors he sells night and day
At the bar of the gin-shop, so glittering and gay.

ANTI-SALOON MESSAGE

the tax. As a result, tax evasion became rampant and col-
lections declined. The tax was reduced in 1868 to the
more reasonable (for those times) level of fifty cents per
gallon.

DEVELOPMENT OF AN OPPOSITION— THE WETS VS. THE DRYS

During the latter half of the nineteenth century, an increasing number of Germans began entering
the country, bringing with them their beer-drinking habits
and beer-making skills. Rapidly after the Civil War, then,
beer came to be the common drink of the common man,
and the mainstay, in the beverage line, of the corner saloon. Just as rapidly, the target of the temperance leaders'
crusade became beer drinking, again associated with the
working-class culture rather than with upper-class culture
where, supposedly, the favored beverages were wines and
brandies. The German segment of the population came to
be continuously associated with the alleged evil, so that
the way was paved during World War I to combine America's hostility to the Germans with the temperance movement's crusade against beer. It is said that our modern
carbonated soft drinks originated during this period, at
the end of the nineteenth century, in response to the temperance movement. Then, "root beer" was invented by
Hires in the hope that it would replace beer as the beverage of the working class.

In 1877, the brewers of the country (mostly German)
recognized the dangers to their trade of the temperance
movement and formed a trade association—the Brewers'
Association—to combat it. They, too, lobbied in legislatures and Congress to offset the influence of the "drys,"

Information Bureau

THE Publicity Department of the National Association of Distillers and Wholesale Dealers conducts an Information Bureau for the purpose of supplying facts, statistics and arguments against Prohibition in whatever way Prohibition may appear.

All questions which may arise in YOUR mind in regard to the Pros and Cons of Prohibition can be answered if you will drop a line to the above department.

Specialists are employed to take care of these requests for information.

Authors and debaters who have in mind proposed discussions on the Pros and Cons of the "Liquor Question" are urged to make use of the special library on this subject available at the offices of the above organization.

Literature dealing with all phases of Prohibition may be obtained free of charge upon application. Requests for special information will be given prompt attention.

Address all communications to "PUBLICITY DEPARTMENT," No. 301 United Bank Building, Cincinnati, Ohio.

OPPOSITION TO PROHIBITION—1880s

thereby acquiring the label of "wets." The brewers utilized the services of a wide network of saloon keepers, reaching into every neighborhood, and they did not hesitate to use both underhanded and straightforward political pressure at the grass-roots level. As a result, the local saloon and the local wardheeler politician became intimately intertwined in a kind of mutual protection arrangement, which rapidly established a strong nucleus and base of operation for grass-roots political action. In some of the big cities it was not uncommon for saloon keepers to control gangs of local thugs who became useful in influencing other people's behavior, including voting behavior. These gangs were the prototypes for the big-city criminal gangs that flourished after World War I. As the brewers' and distillers' power increased through collective efforts, they managed to neutralize the dry crusade for some time to come. The antics of Carrie Nation during this period, for instance, were not so damaging to the saloonkeepers as she hoped, for they converted her efforts to their own interests by mobilizing support among their customers. Also, as the power of the liquor interest grew, through effective political contacts, an increasing lack of respect developed for whatever liquor control laws that did exist (open on Sunday, sales to minors, etc.) and enforcement became increasingly lax. Toward the end of the century, the heavy-handed tactics used by the brewers and distillers began to backfire, earning them increasingly unfavorable publicity. This culminated in a major scandal when the industry sought to buy out certain newspapers in order to have a mouthpiece to state their case to the public.

PRELUDE TO NATIONAL PROHIBITION

In 1874, the WCTU (Women's Christian Temperance Union) was organized in Cleveland by delegates from seventeen states. In 1879, Frances Willard resigned as Dean of Women at Northwestern University to become the head of the organization. She organized branches everywhere throughout the country between 1880 and 1902, enlisting a membership of millions of women.

The Anti-Saloon League also was founded in 1874 as an outgrowth of the former Women's Crusade. After 1895, it grew rapidly in importance and came to be supported by the Catholic Church, whereas the Protestant sects tended to support the WCTU. The organization concentrated on the use of publications to spread its message, established its own publishing house, and by 1912 was turning out forty tons of published material per month. Money was raised by subscriptions from members. In 1926, the organization revealed that it had paid out $25,-000,000 for publications, and by 1914 it was raising $2,500,000 per year from dues.

Various church groups more or less officially signed up with the drys, the first being the General Assembly of the Presbyterian Church in 1854. In 1890, the Southern Baptist and the Christian Church signed up, and in 1892 the Methodist Church became an active supporter of the Anti-Saloon League.

The drys never did take a stand for or against one of the political parties, but gave their support to specific candidates who endorsed their cause. Both the Democratic and Republican parties included a prohibition plank in their platforms after 1900. William Jennings Bryan, in his three bids for the Democratic nomination for president, actively supported the cause.

In 1913, the Anti-Saloon League launched a campaign to
pass an amendment to the federal Constitution to establish nation-wide prohibition. They entered the congressional elections of 1914 in strength, offering many
candidates who claimed to be in sympathy with the movement. The war started then, and even before the U.S.
entered in 1917 a vast amount of national hostility had
built up against anything German. Beer, beer drinking,
and brewers were linked together with the Germans as a
subversive influence. A Senate committee during the war
uncovered evidence that the Brewers' Association had German connections, and the group pleaded guilty to charges
brought against them and paid a fine of $100,000. This
incident largely discredited the "wets'" political influence.

The Congress elected in 1914 passed a prohibition
amendment by a majority of seven, but it needed a two-
thirds majority. Renewed efforts in the 1916 elections to
increase prohibition support were successful. Meanwhile
(1917), a step toward prohibition was achieved when, as
a wartime measure, a law was passed prohibiting the use
of grains for manufacturing whiskey (but not industrial
alcohol, which had by this time become a major industrial
product). In August, 1917, the Eighteenth Amendment
passed Congress with the necessary two-thirds majority
and was submitted to the states for ratification. By January, 1918, the needed thirty-six states had ratified the
amendment. Enabling legislation took the form of the
Volstead Act, passed by Congress in October, 1919. President Wilson thought the Act so poorly written that he ve-
toed it, but it was passed over his veto. The Act placed
enforcement of prohibition laws under the Treasury Department, justified on the obsolete grounds that it was a
revenue act. An ardent prohibitionist, John Kramer, was
appointed as the first director of the prohibition unit and

$2 million were appropriated for carrying out the enforcement program.

PROHIBITION IN OTHER COUNTRIES

Unknown to most Americans is the fact that other countries also experimented with prohibition, nearly always starting off as a wartime measure during World War I, and nearly always ending after a short period of time. Russia, for instance, prohibited the sale and manufacture of vodka during the war, and local governments were given the option of establishing controls over other alcoholic beverages such as wine. Widespread looting of warehouses and liquor dispensing stores followed the passage of the law. The Russians had a long history of attempts on the part of government to obtain revenue by taxing liquor, accompanied by sustained and energetic efforts on the part of citizens to avoid the tax through illegal manufacture and sale.

France and Italy suppressed traffic in absinthe, then prohibited the sale of "spirits" to women and children. As the war progressed, it became illegal to sell "spirits" to soldiers in the combat zones. Germany reduced the brewing of beer to 48 percent, then to 25 percent of prewar consumption in order to conserve barley for bread. Denmark and Switzerland, although neutral during the war, nevertheless experienced shortages, which led to their prohibiting the use of potatoes and corn for distilling liquor. Sweden and Norway empowered the provincial governments to impose absolute prohibition on the sale and manufacture of "spirits" during the war years. Canada, Australia and New Zealand forbade the sale of liquor to soldiers in training, and limited the hours in a day when

sales could be made. England established the Central
Liquor Control Board, which restricted the manufacture
of beer and the release of wines and spirits from bond to
one-half prewar levels.

The national prohibition law in Norway went into effect in 1918 in response to a temperance movement that
got underway during the war years. The manufacture,
sale, and importation of liquors containing more than 14
percent of alcohol were prohibited, thus stimulating both
smuggling and bootlegging. Arrests for drunkenness showed
a steady increase instead of the hoped for decrease. It became evident that prohibition was an unenforceable law,
so a nation-wide plebiscite was held in 1926 and 56 percent of the electorate favored repeal.

The Swedish experience was the only one that could be
regarded as having had some degree of success. The state
took over the distribution and sale of all alcoholic beverages after 1914, and citizens were issued passbooks that
authorized them to buy. To qualify, however, each citizen
had to prove that he had paid all taxes and was not an
alcoholic. With some modifications, the Swedish plan is
still in effect.

THE EMOTIONAL CLIMATE
SURROUNDING THE ONSET OF
PROHIBITION

Americans today are generally unaware of the
intense and pervasive hostility that was expressed toward
anything German during World War I, because during
World War II the animosity was directed chiefly toward
Hitler and Nazism rather than toward the German people
or German traditions. In the first war, however, every-

thing German was portrayed as an evil and accepted as such by the people. German operas were banned, the German language ceased being taught in many high schools, and sauerkraut came to be called "liberty cabbage." The Kaiser was looked upon as the personification of evil. Atrocity stories coming from England and France when these countries stood alone against the Germans were accepted without question. German scientific and industrial advances were widely discredited, even though they had been held in high esteem before the war. Medical journals, for example, sought to discredit German medical advances during this time and justified their stance on the grounds that Germans were inhuman and barbarous. Americans with German names fell victim to discrimination, and many Anglicized their names in response.

The United States entered the war relatively late, and engaged in actual military efforts for only about a year. Perhaps because of this timing, our ventures seemed to be an immediate and unadulterated success. The people of the country were well organized to support the war effort, which rapidly took on the aura of a great crusade. People competed with one another to show their patriotism by offering to make great sacrifices for the war effort. Actually, there were few significant shortages during the war, but people prided themselves on going without sugar or coffee, for instance, because these commodities were expected to be in short supply.

When the Armistice was signed in November, 1918, the enthusiasm and eagerness to support the war was still growing. The end of the war brought about a great sense of moral victory, and, at that moment, the United States might be said to have become a grownup among nations. The general belief was that American idealism had triumphed over European moral decadence. With it all, the

United States had largely profited from the war, and had sustained remarkably little damage, as compared with the devastation to which England, France, and Germany had been subjected. In short, when the war was over there still existed in the country a vast, unexpended fervor still looking for causes. In this atmosphere of great righteousness the passing of the laws establishing national prohibition became yet another expression of national moral pride.

Some other factors also crept into the picture at the close of the war. For instance, the women's suffrage movement had acquired a great deal of momentum, and had been encouraged by the temperance movement, which was widely regarded as a successful female effort. Moreover, women soon would acquire the right to vote and began entering college in large numbers, going into business and professional careers and taking on such formerly non-feminine habits as smoking and drinking. Working-class unrest leading to violent riots and demonstrations of considerable violence spread through the major industrial cities. These outbreaks were blamed on the "bolshevists", anarchists, radicals, socialists, the I.W.W. (International Workers of the World), and other unions. The incidents and the scapegoats created from them led to the United States' long pre-occupation with the "communist menace." In retrospect, it now appears clear that this period of history represents a revolution in our development. Strong forces for change were countered with strong forces to maintain the status quo. The predominantly agrarian society that the United States had been and that still existed as the idyllic American image had been transformed into an industrial society. The inferiority complex that previously had characterized the nation's view of itself in relation to the family of nations was suddenly transformed into an arrogant

THE UNLICENSED ROBBER.

Highwayman: "*Your money OR your life.*"

THE LICENSED ROBBER.

Rumseller: "*Your money AND your life.*"

ANTI-SALOON MESSAGE

superiority. The refined and artistic culture of Europe, which had previously made the U.S. look like a barren wilderness, suddenly was decaying and dying, making our culture look, instead, young, vigorous, and pure.

The great sense of confidence gained from victory in the war, with its underlying sense of right triumphant, imbued the country with the notion that the best way to solve problems was the American way, a direct approach. All agreed, for instance, that drinking represented a problem, one that was highlighted by the growing industrialization of the nation in which a drunken workman posed the threat of inefficiency and demoralization. The direct approach to the problem seemed obvious—make the manufacture and sale of alcoholic beverages illegal. The self-denial this might entail to the non-alcoholic seemed to be offset by the continuing wartime attitude of self-sacrifice and the great sense of moral righteousness arising from the sacrifice and victory.

AMERICANA OF THE TWENTIES

The end of the war ushered in a new cultural era that truly represented the transition between a more traditional and familiar kind of culture to the ultra-technological culture we have today. As a transitional period, it was filled with wild fluctuations, new standards of conduct, new patterns of living, and a substantial degree of confusion with which people were extraordinarily comfortable. The old style, which underwent a progressive decline, was basically a lower-middle-class, Anglo-Saxon, Protestant type, having roots in a "back home on the farm" kind of nostalgia. The old pioneering spirit and frontier attitudes still lingered, along with a heavy touch of puritanism in lower-class circles and Victorianism in upper circles, both adding up to a tendency to disparage pleasure and honor hard work. Another frontier concept still strong was that each individual was quite capable of governing himself and did not need a set of rules from society or the government to guide him. Fair play, honesty in business dealings, sympathy for the underdog, and contempt for hypocrisy and the accouterments of power prevailed. Notably absent was any significant non-Anglo-Saxon influence brought to the country by the millions of southern Europeans who immigrated during the fifty years preceding World War I. Instead, these people became Americanized.

Chapter

2

PROHIBITION ARRIVES– THE NOBLE EXPERIMENT

THE LAW

THE Volstead Act defined an alcoholic beverage as one having no more than ½ percent alcohol, thus eliminating wine and beer from the exempted class, an exemption favored by many people opposing prohibition. Only "near beer" was legal. Near beer was made in the same way as regular beer, but then was diluted with water to reduce the alcohol concentration to an insignificant level. Some breweries continued in business in order to produce near beer, but it was never very popular. A few distilleries were licensed to continue in business, although most closed down. Those remaining in business produced distilled liquors to be sold through drug stores, and then to patients on a doctor's prescription for "medicinal purposes." "Sacramental" wines were permitted to be sold to ordained clergyman of those religious sects that used such wines (mostly Catholics and Jews). The homeowner was permitted to brew his own beer or ferment his own wine, but he could not operate a still to make alcohol. It was clearly not appreciated at the time of the passage of the laws how large the production of industrial alcohol was and how identical the process was (and is) to the manufacture of whiskey. Industrial alcohol was required to be "denatured" in order to make it unfit for human consumption, and a number of different formulas was used for denaturing purposes, some more lethal than others. Nevertheless, industrial alcohol was diverted into beverage channels in large quantities. Otherwise, the manufacture, distribution, importation, and sale of alcoholic beverages was prohibited.

It was apparently assumed, but not emphasized by the prohibitionists, that a major share of the enforcement problems would be borne by local and state officials. However, the major part of the enforcement responsibility even-

AMERICA'S MISSION

"My fellow countrymen, the armistice was signed this morning. Everything for which America fought has been accomplished. It will now be our fortunate duty to assist by example, by sober friendly counsel, and by material aid in the establishment of just democracy throughout the world."

President Wilson's Proclamation of the Armistice, November 11, 1918.

"Now that liberty has triumphed, now that the forces of Right have begun their reconstruction of humanity's morals, the world faces a material task of equal magnitude."

From a Newspaper the Same Day.

tually fell to the federal government. No appreciable
pressure was placed on the states to share the burden.

The Volstead Act had been drafted by the Anti-Saloon
League and showed no awareness of the problems of enforcement. It received only a few hours' debate in Congress
before passage and was subsequently passed again over
President Wilson's veto. There never had been much prohibition sentiment in the major big cities of the country,
especially cities like New York, Philadelphia, Boston, Bal-
timore, Chicago, and New Orleans. Mild protests over the
passage of the Act arose in these centers, but otherwise
everybody else in the country seemed ready to acclaim it
as a great victory for old-fashioned, puritanical morality,
a quality of American life that just happened to expire at
about the same time. In a sense, the Act and the Eighteenth
Amendment provided a peculiar sense of satisfaction for
millions of people still seeking ways of supporting the
great crusade against the Germans. On the one hand, they
could wholeheartedly endorse the move on the grounds
that drinking was a self-evident evil—in other people, that
is—while serenely disregarding it because they never
meant the restrictions to apply to themselves. This same
sentiment prevailed throughout the prohibition era. It was
apparently assumed that the mere shutting down of distilleries and breweries would automatically stop the flow
of liquor and eliminate the problem of drinking. No one
in 1919 seemed to realize that industrial alcohol was the
same as whiskey except for the container in which it was
sold.

In any event, the enforcement of the law was placed in
the hands of the Treasury Department, which was given
an appropriation of $2 million for the purpose. In 1920,
Congress provided for 1,520 agents to be hired by the prohibition enforcement unit in the Treasury, but refused to

THE EIGHTEENTH AMENDMENT

1. After one year from the ratification of this article the manufacture, sale or transportation of intoxicating liquors within, the importation thereof from the United States and all territory subject to the jurisdiction thereof for beverage purposes is hereby prohibited.

2. The Congress and the several states shall have concurrent power to enforce this article by appropriate legislation.

3. This article shall be inoperative unless it shall have been ratified as an amendment to the Constitution by the legislatures of the several states, as provided in the Constitution, within seven years from the date of the submission hereof to the states by the Congress.

Proposed in the Congress by resolution on December 18, 1917. Declared ratified by three-fourths of the states on January 16, 1919. Went into effect one year later, on January 16, 1920.

place them under civil service, thus making them political jobs. The salaries of the agents originally ranged from $1,200 to $2,000, thus eliminating the possibility of recruiting any kind of experts and making the agents vulnerable to corruption. There never arose any great pressure to increase the manpower, and by 1930 the number of agents had increased only to 2,836, although pressure did develop later on to convert them to civil service status and transfer them to the Department of Justice, both of which finally happened.

Beginning immediately after the Volstead Act went into effect, and continuing throughout the prohibition era, the

Department of Agriculture issued many helpful publications on how to make wines, beers, and spirits. Stores sprang up immediately to supply a demand that rapidly blossomed for hops, yeast, malt, copper tubing, barrels, bottling equipment, and the like. Hip flasks were quickly invented and quickly became universally available. The government issued many warnings about the use of home stills for the distillation of alcohol, and required that a person purchasing one had to sign an affidavit that he did not intend to use it for this purpose. Nevertheless, there was essentially no interference with the home industry that developed, as long as it did not lead to sales outside the home.

TRIUMPH OF THE PROHIBITIONISTS

BILLY SUNDAY's "ORATION FOR JOHN BARLEYCORN'S FUNERAL"

"Good-bye John. You were God's worst enemy. You were Hell's best friend. The reign of tears is over. The slums soon will be only a memory, we will turn our prisons into factories and our jails into storehouses and corncribs. Men will walk upright now, women will smile, and the children will laugh. Hell will be forever for rent."

From Paul Sann, The Lawless Decade (New York: Bonanza Books, 1942).

The standard American saloon was closed down all over the country, and with it were closed many of the famous old restaurants that had sold liquor, such as Delmonico's in New York City. In their place, of course, a much greater number of "speakeasies" opened up. The stage for prohibition was set during the closing days of 1919 when the sale of liquor was still permitted but distilleries and breweries were closed. Either real or imagined shortages (there were still vast stores of whiskey in bonded warehouses) pushed up prices and led to a growing conviction on the part of customers that liquor was going to be difficult to obtain.

ENFORCEMENT

The Volstead Act went into effect on January 16, 1920. By this time, most of the great sense of righteousness that accompanied its passage had largely evaporated, to be replaced by new demands on citizens' ingenuity in finding new sources of supply once the old sources had been stopped. There appears to have been no long waiting period before this ingenuity became expressed in a long list of ways by which all kinds of alcoholic beverages continued to be available. The large eastern cities led the way in early active defiance of the law, for there the sympathy for the prohibition cause was minimal. Arrests for violations were made within a few days, and one of the earliest scandals was the seizure of a still on the Texas farm of the congressman who wrote the Eighteenth Amendment—all within the first week.

A survey of the different attitudes concerning enforcement can now be retrospectively made with some assurance of its validity. The congressmen who voted for prohibition legislation did so, apparently, only to get the votes of the drys, which had become substantial in number. Having thus appeased these constituents, they saw no

FORGOTTEN PROHIBITIONS OF THE NOT-TOO-DISTANT PAST

Kansas: A bill is before the Legislature to make the possession of cigarettes an offense punishable by imprisonment. Kansas already has a law against selling or giving away cigarettes, but not against smoking them.

Utah: Four men were arrested for smoking in a Salt Lake City cafe. Utah has a law prohibiting smoking in public and the sale of cigarettes.

Connecticut: A bill is before the Legislature to make the public display of a clock showing any time except Eastern Standard Time punishable by $100 or ten days in prison.

New York: A hearing is now going on to amend the state laws (already in force) against disseminating contraceptive information. If the bill is enacted, it will be a victory for Mrs. Margaret Sanger, one of the world's leading birth control advocates.

Connecticut: The Legislature defeated a bill to legalize Sunday football and baseball.

Pennsylvania: A bill to prohibit any municipality from adopting Daylight Saving Time was passed by the Legislature.

Washington, D.C.: By decision of the Attorney General, it is no longer illegal for women to wear trousers.

From Time *magazine's review of newsworthy legislation for the year 1923.*

need to do any more, and, as a result, subsequent congressional activities concerning enforcement virtually lapsed until President Roosevelt mobilized support to obtain repeal. The federal administration apparently saw the legislation for what it was to the legislators who passed it instead of what it meant to the citizens who had demanded it. It was regarded, in other words, as a political whim of expediency that would soon die of neglect and be forgotten. None of the next few presidents (Harding, Coolidge, Hoover) made much of it as a problem. The states and local governments saw the legislation as a set of restrictions imposed on the citizens by the federal government, which although popular enough during the fight for passage, was bound to be unpopular when it came to enforcement. They, therefore, relied almost exclusively on federal agents and courts to take responsibility for enforcement. The drys remained so righteously triumphant with their success and so captivated with the thought of the great transformations that would take place in society now that prohibition was a reality that they consistently blinded themselves to the problem of enforcement. To them, any admission that enforcement was a difficult problem was tantamount to an admission of defeat, so they continued to be optimistic about the promise of prohibition. The wets, meanwhile, usually quietly and sometimes noisily, bided their time, knowing that American enterprise would not fail to supply the market they represented. Throughout the twenties, public sentiment appeared to be in favor of prohibition as a national policy, in spite of the lack of support for it as a practice, and any arguments by the wets to the contrary were construed as unpatriotic.

Almost immediately, there was rampant violation of the new laws, and open defiance of the law became a conspicuous thrust in the new cultural patterns that began to emerge. As in the early Georgia experiment, the violators seemed to feel little or no personal guilt. Drinking patterns and habits were markedly changed, not the least of which was the wide-spread entry of women on the social-drinking scene. Even stealing liquor became an acceptable activity. The "flapper age," gangsterism, the speakeasy, and

RUMRUNNING IN 1925

Attorney General Stone made public statistical data on numbers of foreign vessels engaged in organized liquor smuggling into the US:

British vessels	307
Norwegian	10
French vessels	4
Others	11
Total	332

As many as 63 of these ships have been known to be off our coast at one time, waiting to transship their cargoes into small boats that usually do the smuggling.

From Time *magazine's summary of news in 1925.*

the bootlegger became new social fixtures, many destructive effects of which are still apparent (organized crime).

In spite of the great increase in court loads, there were no provisions made for expanding the legal apparatus to handle violators. Later in the twenties, a governor of New York, in commenting on the state's failure to participate actively in enforcement, estimated that diligent efforts in that direction would require one-third of the state's citizens to apprehend another third who were violators, while the remaining third would be tied up serving on juries.

Between 1920 and 1924, the population of the federal prisons doubled, most of the new inmates being violators of the Volstead Act. In 1928, the peak year, 75,000 arrests were made and in 1928 convictions rose to 58,000. An average of 25,000 cases were pending in the courts at the end of each year. A survey in New York in 1923 indicated that of 6,900 arrests, only 20 were brought to trial and 496 pleaded guilty without a trial. The typical case brought to court—usually for bootlegging—pleaded guilty and paid a fine of $100. In 1928, 44 percent of federal attorneys' time was spent on liquor violators.

When courts became so congested with cases that the situation became intolerable, the Department of Justice began holding "bargain days"—days set aside when violators were allowed to plead guilty *en masse* and be let free with a fine.

After 1921, the federal agents began using the "padlock," whereby a speakeasy found to be selling liquor (and perhaps not paying off the police or being subjected to complaints from competitors) would, without due process, be closed down for a prescribed period of time. Numerous stories circulated about agents failing to obtain search warrants, using unnecessary violence in prosecutions, and other arbitrary tactics. Until 1930, when they were transferred to the Justice Department, the only qualification for prohibition agents was that they be certified members of the political party in power. Their low salaries opened the way to widespread bribery. After a while, it was not uncommon for the major enforcement thrust to be directed toward only certain members of a competing group of bootleggers, thus serving the interests of the remainder. Within ten days after the Volstead Act went into effect, three agents were indicted for accepting bribes in Chicago and in December, 1921, the New York City office fired 100 agents for fraud. In 1925, forty-eight agents were convicted of conspiracy at one time, and during the first four years of prohibition, 141 agents were jailed. By 1926, 10,000 agents had served in the 2,200 jobs, and by 1930 there had been a total turnover of 17,816, of which 11,926 had been fired. New York and Pennsylvania each had six different state directors in three and a half years, each one being indicted for conspiracy. Later, during the hearings of the Wickersham Commission (appointed by President Hoover to investigate the enforcement problem), a few, apparently honest, agents reported that they had been offered 373 bribes, totaling $90,000. One agent also reported that he had been offered a total of $15,000,000 over a year's period to permit a brewery to set up operations. President Harding stated, in 1922, only two years after the onset of the Noble Experiment, that the situation was already "a nation-wide scandal and the most demoralizing factor in public life." However, he did nothing about it. Not until Hoover's election in 1928 did the problem become a campaign issue.

Several efforts to bring enforcement personnel under civil service standards failed until 1927 when a bill to that effect was finally passed. Then, few applicants could be found who could pass the qualifying examinations. After two years, only two-thirds of the employees had qualified, and others were recruited to fill the rest of the jobs.

It was decided early that federal property would be exempted from searches for illegal liquor, thus providing a neat sanctuary for the illegal liquor traffic. A congressman was convicted and sent to prison for accepting a bribe of $5,000 to release liquor from a bonded warehouse. Nevertheless, he ran for re-election and was supported, this time by the Anti-Saloon League on the basis of his voting record favoring prohibition. This incident was typical of many that occurred, but the implications of all this seemed to escape most people. Some of the most ardent supporters of restrictive legislation were the ones who profited from those restrictions. Similarly, the most avid opponents of any given smuggler or bootlegger turned out to be his competitors in the same business, who could often be depended on to produce the evidence needed for convictions.

The Coast Guard also became involved in the corruption. It was not unknown for rumrunners to be escorted into safe harbor by Coast Guard boats. The entire crews of two boats were convicted of conspiracy and the commanding officer of a Coast Guard station in Rhode Island was indicted for smuggling.

In New Orleans, in 1925, the Controller of Customs, the police captain, a sheriff, a senator's brother, and twenty-seven other officials were indicted on charges of conspiracy. In Buffalo, a port of entry for liquor from Canada, the Chief Immigration Officer was indicted. In Detroit, probably the most active port of entry for Canadian merchandise, one hundred federal agents, in 1929, were found to be on the payrolls of the smugglers. The investigation disclosed that a standard price had been established for payoffs ($1.87 per case of whiskey) and the smugglers who were apprehended from time to time invariably turned out to be those who refused to pay the federal agents. As early as 1921, twenty-three county officials in Fayette County, Pennsylvania, were accused by a grand jury of extortion in connection with payoffs from bootleggers. In 1923, seventy-five citizens of Gary, Indiana, including all the city officials, were arrested simultaneously for violations. In 1924, the mayor of Philadelphia requested help from the federal government to break the power of the liquor interests, and a detachment of Marines under the command of General Smedley Butler confidently undertook the assignment. The General imposed military discipline on the police force and began a series of dramatic raids. After a few months, however, he admitted defeat and quietly withdrew.

Nevertheless, in 1922, Haynes, the new Commissioner of the Prohibition Unit, praised the new era of "clean living" that had prevailed since prohibition had gone into effect and stated that there were no significant enforcement problems. He claimed, for instance, that 17,500,000 former alcoholics had given up drinking, thus making the whole experiment worthwhile. This blindness to reality was echoed many times later during the twenties and has continued to be the dominant theme in the drug enforcement area today. Throughout both the alcohol and the drug prohibition eras, there has been a perpetual tendency for leaders in the enforcement area to misconstrue good intentions as actual practice.

In 1918, there had been 8,168 licensed saloons in New York City, which were closed when the Volstead Act went into effect in 1920. By 1926, a government survey estimated that 100,000 speakeasies had taken their place, and the police had actual records of the existence of 32,000 of them. In 1929 alone, 18,589 owners of speakeasies were arrested but typically paid small fines and then moved their place of business to a new location. At one time, in 1925, the Treasury Department actually opened its own speakeasy in New York City, for the alleged purpose of using it as a way of making contact with the powerful illegal liquor interests. It was eventually disclosed, however, that the business was so well organized that the speakeasy manager had contact only with salesmen and minor delivery men. The government found it very difficult to justify this move when news of it finally came to public attention.

The standard price of a drink of whiskey in a licensed

saloon before prohibition was 15 cents. In speakeasies, by 1920, the price had risen to between 40 cents and 60 cents. In the big cities, which had both the best and the worst in the way of elaborate accommodations in speakeasies, prices were as low as 10 cents for what was probably nothing but denatured alcohol and as high as $1.00 for good Scotch subjected to an unknown degree of dilution. The "good stuff" obtained from bonded warehouse supplies or from smuggling operations was usually diluted four or five times with either water or alcohol before sale. A lucrative market developed for used bottles in which moonshine could be bottled as "good stuff," and well-known whiskey labels were counterfeited and sold. A rash of books was published to provide a curious public with the technical knowledge needed to pursue these ingenious schemes.

SOURCES OF SUPPLY

Few challenges to American entrepreneurial enterprise were met with more skilled and prompt response than the task of developing new, extra-legal sources of supply and channels of distribution to satisfy the nation's demand for alcoholic beverages. In most cases, the channels were well developed long before the enforcement officials were prepared to plug them, so that it is safe to say that no appreciable inroads were made in stopping up any of the various sources.

At the onset of prohibition in 1920, there were 69,000,000 gallons of whiskey stored in bonded government warehouses. Although under the Treasury Department's supervision, this liquor was owned by the distillers. Four distilleries were allowed to continue in operation to replenish the supplies in the warehouses as they were de-

pleted, and it was assumed that all this liquor would be
distributed through the "legitimate" channel of "medicinal
whiskey" through drugstores by doctor's prescription. By
1921, the amount distributed this way amounted to 8,000,-
000 gallons per year. Physicians were not allowed to write
more than 100 prescriptions every 90 days. Bootleggers
managed to set up phony drugstores (apparently as many
as 3,300 of them) to get this legal allotment, although unlike the ethical drugstores they typically diluted theirs as
much as four to one with water. Counterfeit prescriptions
were widely sold, and, when a count was later made, a
substantially larger number of official prescription forms
were turned in than had originally been issued. One-hun-
dred thousand physicians—a great majority of the physicians in the nation—obtained the special license needed
to issue these prescriptions. It was not unusual for physicians to sell the prescriptions outright, on the open market. In one city, it is reported, the competition among
physicians became so intense that the price fell to 25 cents
each. A lawyer in Chicago is reported to have made a
profit of $5,000,000 by buying 890 barrels of Jack Daniels'
bourbon for $125,000 for a dummy drugstore he had set
up. The licensed distillers appear to have manufactured
much more whiskey than entered legal channels, the remainder being siphoned off by highjacking. Highjacking
whiskey became widespread, and anyone daring to transport a shipment had to take a substantial risk. The prevalence of highjacking also provided a convenient excuse for
accounting for inventory discrepancies, and chances are
that some of the so-called highjackers were really subsidiary distribution channels. Another link in the distribution
system that permitted diversions of legal merchandise into
illegal channels was the wholesalers who were licensed to
handle bonded whiskey. Again, it became possible to set

up dummy companies to operate such warehouses solely for the illegal trade, although dealing in legal merchandise.

Industrial alcohol became a fairly important product of the growing chemical industry in the U.S. As we have mentioned, few people then, and probably equally few today, appreciate that "grain alcohol"—that is to say, ethyl alcohol—is made in essentially the same way as is whiskey. Molasses and other sugar products have long been the preferred raw materials for fermentation, after which they are distilled into alcohol, or rum. When prohibition went into effect, about 7,000,000 gallons of industrial alcohol were manufactured annually. The new laws provided that this alcohol be denatured before being sold, and to accomplish this, a variety of "formulas" was used to make it unsuitable for human consumption. As prohibition wore on, these formulas became increasingly difficult to separate from the raw alcohol, but early in the prohibition era it was not difficult to separate them. As a result, a great deal was purchased legally and reprocessed to make what was claimed to be potable alcohol. Varying amounts of other substances having more or less disastrous effects on humans could often be found in the product, however. There was no tax on this denatured alcohol, so it could be obtained quite cheaply. Typically, it was marketed as gin, and thus began the new gin-drinking culture. It was so often contaminated with impurities that fouled its taste that the custom rapidly developed of mixing it with various flavoring materials to make it more pleasant. Thus, the cocktail was established as a drinking fixture. Ginger ale, for instance, became popular as a flavoring at this time.

Another common way of directing industrial alcohol into the bootlegging trade was through the process of buying out or setting up a company that purported to manufacture products such as shaving lotion or flavoring

extracts of which alcohol was a component. Thus, legal
supplies could be obtained. These practices also informed
the American public about the many products on the market that contained legal alcohol (canned heat, shaving lotion, flavoring extracts, shoe polish) and many Americans
were foolhardy enough to consume them without any modification. Various wild claims were made for ways of ex-
tracting pure alcohol from these substances, and the skid
row alcoholic, particularly, became a frequent poisoning
victim as a result. One such theory claimed that denatured
alcohol, such as is used as an anti-freeze in autos, could
be detoxified by percolating it through a loaf of bread.
Some denaturing plants did a fairly good job of chemically
removing the denaturing components of industrial alcohol.
The prohibition director of New York in 1928 estimated
that there were sixteen full-scale denaturing plants in operation near New York City, turning out 11,000,000 gallons
annually. The U.S. attorney in New York estimated that,
in Pennsylvania, the retail value of liquor made from industrial alcohol was $3.6 billion per year.

"Near beer" was legal beer, meaning that it had less
than ½ percent alcohol. Although most of the pre-prohibition breweries closed down during prohibition, some remained open to produce this beverage, and new ones were
opened to produce either near beer, or illegal, regular 6
percent beer. Near beer was made by simply diluting ordinary 6 percent beer with water, and never proved to be
very popular. However, it served to be very useful as a
front to conceal the sale of regular beer. Unless an un-
corrupted federal agent was actually present at the time
the dilution took place (and this was unlikely), it became
a rather simple matter to bottle or barrel the straight stuff
and ship it to a willing customer. Similarly, at the retail
outlet, it became relatively easy to appear to be selling

near beer while the better grade was available, unless the customer happened to be a federal agent. As organized bootleggers acquired power and extensive outlets in the big cities, they opened their own breweries to supply the trade. It was found that the cost of brewing a keg of beer was about $1.00 and it could be sold for as much as $25 wholesale; and at the rate of 25 cents to 50 cents per glass, it brought as much as $100 retail. When General Butler took the Marines to Philadelphia to enforce the prohibition laws, he found thirteen breweries in business, although technically they had been closed down. Even he failed to get them closed.

Wine had never been a very popular beverage in the U.S., but prohibition became responsible for creating a major California grape and wine industry. The Volstead Act permitted a citizen to ferment as much as 200 gallons of wine per year, but he was not permitted to sell it. Acreage planted in grapes in California rose from 97,000 in 1919 to 680,000 in 1926 to meet the demand that developed for wine. The growers marketed their product first as grape juice, and later through the ingenious device of vacuum-dried grape bricks which were more economical to ship. Conveniently, they sometimes labeled their product with a dire warning of what could happen if certain steps were taken—namely, those steps needed to convert the bricks into wine. These warnings made very handy recipes. Sometimes the juice was marketed in kegs that were already suited to the process of fermentation.

Wines were legally produced to supply the sacramental wine market. The law provided that these wines could be sold only to authentic priests and rabbis, and at a rate of 1 gallon per parisioner per year. Soon, spurious priests and rabbis with fictitious "congregations" were setting themselves up in business.

Smuggling was always a time-honored American type of enterprise, having had its origin in colonial days when England sought to impose import restrictions on the colonists. Maine's long experience with prohibition had already developed a well-organized system of distribution from Canada. Almost the minute prohibition took effect, ships from the Caribbean and from Europe began making runs to the U.S. with cargoes of what came to be the highly esteemed "good stuff," such as Scotch and brandies. These ships anchored outside the territorial limits and sold their cargoes directly to small boats from the mainland. These craft then tried to outwit and outrace the Coast Guard in order to reach port safely. The major landings of large cargoes of "good stuff" destined for the fancy speakeasies in New York were regularly reported in the newspapers. At the beginning, before the Coast Guard was fully mobilized to deal with the smuggling problem, both amateur and professional rumrunners entered the trade; but as it became more difficult to cope with the Coast Guard, the amateurs disappeared. The professionals reached such a point of power and affluence that they chartered their own ships to bring in entire shiploads from foreign ports. One wholesaler, for instance, was known to have brought in a shipment costing him $850,000, but worth many times that amount on the retail market. Actually, the "good stuff" was cut with either alcohol or water, so consistently, in fact, that the drinking public lost its ability to recognize unadulterated Scotch. The rumrunners probably did much to encourage and advance some of the new technologies becoming available, such as shortwave radio and outboard motors.

Smuggling from Canada was particularly attractive because no problems would arise until the smuggler reached the border. The government of Canada imposed no obstacles; as a matter of fact, it issued weekly reports of the amounts of liquor sold to Americans. The thousands of miles of border, the hundreds of roads crossing the border, and the open waters of the Great Lakes provided many avenues for smuggling. Air freight may well have been invented in October, 1921 when an airplane carried the first cargo of booze from Winnipeg to the states. By 1930, regular air runs had been established. Railroads that crossed the border also served as a convenient link in the distribution system. A favorite device was to use lines that originated in the U.S., crossed the border into Canada, and then ran back into the U.S. (e.g., New York to Ontario to Michigan). A cargo of boxes filled with empty bottles would be shipped from the U.S., filled with liquor in Canada, then routed to another U.S. destination, apparently with a cargo originating from the U.S. By 1925, it was estimated that 800 boats were making regular runs across the Great Lakes. On the Canadian side of the Detroit River, there were eighty-three breweries and distilleries serving the demand. Detroit became the principal port of entry.

The art of distilling whiskey outside of legal commercial channels (moonshine) was a well-developed part of American folklore, and is still. In the short period between 1921 and 1925, 696,933 stills were confiscated by federal agents. The manufacture of moonshine was originally confined to the mountain regions and rather remote rural areas, but later spread to the cities. Many downtown areas in the U.S. came to be known for the perpetual aroma of fermenting mash that hung in the atmosphere. In the Middle West, enterprising organizations developed networks of local farmers who manufactured moonshine for a syndicate that collected it regularly and sold it in the big cities such as St. Louis. It was occasionally reported that coercive means were used to induce farmers to join these cooperatives. Little effort was made to stamp out these sources. One gang in Indiana was known to have thirty-seven stills in operation, producing 1,000 gallons per day. Twenty-nine members of this gang were arrested and convicted.

In big cities, police protection was needed to operate a still for they were rather difficult to conceal. It was said that a capital investment of $250,000 could turn out 15,000 gallons per day. As powerful organizations got into the distribution end (bootlegging) of the business, it became easy for small operators to obtain loans or equipment from the bootleggers to set up production units. One of the nagging problems was finding means of disposing of the used, fermented mash. It tended to clog up sewers, for instance. It was not uncommon, after federal raids on these stills were made, to publicize findings that might have been true, or that might have been invented to disillusion the public. Reports of finding all kinds of garbage and dead animals in the fermenting mash were typical, but there is little to indicate that this kind of unfavorable publicity hurt the retail business.

TYPES OF ALCOHOLIC BEVERAGES AVAILABLE

As mentioned above, imported Canadian whiskey, Scotch, and French wines and brandies were the most highly prized kinds of drinks sold, but they were rarely sold in their unadulterated state. The liquor was sent to "cutting houses" for dilution, and required extra bottles, preferably those with standard labels and design. The final retail price came to $100 per case. The best source of reasonably "good stuff" was near the Canadian border, for although the smuggled merchandise reached all parts of the country, it tended to undergo increasing degrees of adulteration with distance from the border.

Raw alcohol from various sources, the common one being industrial alcohol (denatured, and then reprocessed), became the common raw material for making all kinds of novel drinks and substitutes for traditional ones. Industrial alcohol could be bought for twenty cents per gallon. Various substances were added to alcohol to give it an acceptable flavor, and gin became the standby of both the bootlegger and the home processor. Scotch was simulated by adding glycerine and iodine to alcohol. The mixed drink, the cocktail, achieved its current popularity in an effort to disguise unpleasant tastes with various flavorings.

Moonshine whiskey was, ideally, bourbon, and occasionally reached the quality expected of good bourbons, but this goal was most often sabotaged by the general reluctance to allow time for the necessary aging. More often, moonshine was made of anything that could be fermented and distilled, with no quality controls exercised in the process.

Wood alcohol was a common ingredient in the chemical industry, used as a solvent, and often turned up in the bootlegged products sold to the public. A government laboratory once reported that analysis of several samples of confiscated moonshine contained significant amounts of wood alcohol. In 1928, there were sixty deaths attributed to wood alcohol. A newspaper in New York City obtained samples of drinks sold in speakeasies, had them analyzed, and reported that 57 of 504 contained as much as 3 percent wood alcohol.

The skid row alcoholic especially consumed products not

meant for consumption because they contained wood alcohol—toilet water, canned heat, bay rum, perfume, hair tonic, and rubbing alcohol.

Farm laborers, especially in the Midwest, discovered that molasses used in making silage fermented and accumulated at the bottom of silos as an alcoholic liquid. Thus, a drink of dubious quality but of certain alcoholic content became freely available on the farms.

Late during prohibition, fluid extract of Jamaica ginger was discovered. It was 90 percent alcohol, but contained a rather lethal component that produced the conditions which came to be known as "Jake's paralysis." In 1930, a report claimed to have identified 15,000 victims of the extract.

Estimates of the amount of alcohol consumed during prohibition varied widely, depending on the bias of the reporter—whether a wet or a dry. The Anti-Saloon League and the Prohibition Bureau continuously produced optimistic reports. Licensed whiskey sold by prescription through physicians finally was measured. In 1930, 159,000 prescriptions were issued by 70,000 physicians, which would have accounted for 991,000 gallons taken from bond. Actually, 1,400,000 gallons were sold from bond, the difference presumably attributable to counterfeit prescriptions.

Perhaps the most reliable drink sold illegally was beer, made in the standard fashion, and subjected to at least elementary quality control because of the competition. The fundamental crusade of the prohibitionists had been to stamp out the traditional saloon with its reputation of providing headquarters for various sinful activities. The speakeasies that replaced the saloons not only outnumbered them by a large margin, but also housed far more questionable activities. The awareness of this turn of events never seemed to have a bearing on the continued efforts to support prohibition. Here again, good intentions seemed to be enough to justify the crusade, and the same lack of insight tends to color the current campaign against drugs.

REPEAL

The prohibition issue entered a presidential campaign for the first time in 1928 when Al Smith, the Democratic candidate, took a stand for repeal of the Eighteenth Amendment. By this time, some compromises had been proposed, the principal one being to modify the definition of an alcoholic beverage in the Volstead Act by permitting the sale of wines and beer. Another compromise endorsed the principle of making prohibition a matter for each state to decide for itself. Hoover was assumed to be a supporter of prohibition, although his strongest statement in this regard was his referral to prohibition as a "great social experiment." The 1928 campaign took place during the rising tide of business prosperity and the wild speculation that was then gripping Wall Street and the nation. The Republicans took credit for the alleged state of prosperity, on the grounds that it had exercised minimal restraints on business. Probably because of this claim, rather than because of many votes that Smith lost because of his Catholicism, Hoover won. However, he promptly appointed the Wickersham Commission to investigate the problem of enforcement. The Commission took its job very seriously, and the report it produced several years later was highly critical of the enforcement efforts.

By 1930, the American Legion supported repeal, and the American Bar Association adopted a resolution calling for repeal. In 1929, the Women's Organization for National

Prohibition Reform, organized by the Republican National Committee, took the repeal stand, and for the first time added women's voices to the opposition to prohibition. A Moderation League was organized by a group of very prominent corporate executives in a rational effort to introduce the notion that compromise might offer new and better solutions. The president of the DuPont Corporation, for instance, claimed that repeal could eliminate the income tax because of the revenues that could be generated by taxing legal alcohol.

The stock market crash of 1929 and the depression that followed crystallized the nation's disillusionment toward all the policies that had prevailed during the twenties—Republicanism and prohibition being the chief targets. The desperate state of the economy and the despair that prevailed in the land made almost any kind of change seem desirable. Roosevelt campaigned on the "wet" platform, and quickly kept his campaign promise when elected in 1932 to first repeal the Volstead Act (permitting the sale of 3.2 percent beer) and then the Eighteenth Amendment in 1934. When Roosevelt signed the proclamation ending prohibition (national, that is, it still persisted in some states), he expressed the hope that the states would prevent the return of the saloons.

Chapter

3

THE NEW AMERICAN CULTURE

CAUSES AND SYMPTOMS

THE revolutionary changes that occurred in American culture during the post World War I period cannot be attributed to prohibition in a cause-and-effect relationship. Instead, it would seem more rational to view the phenomenon of the twenties as it was related to the widespread defiance of the laws as merely a symptom of the prevailing changes. Nevertheless, much of what characterizes the period can be epitomized by what happened to prohibition. In a sense, the prohibition laws represented, for the times, an embodiment of an old set of values that was in the process of being overthrown, but in the process of being abandoned was enthroned on a pedestal as a highly conspicuous symbol of past tradition. Meanwhile, the actual practices of the times followed an opposite extreme, not only as an open and widespread defiance of the old tradition but also in an exuberant joyfulness in doing so.

GROWTH OF THE AMERICAN CULTURE DURING THE TWENTIETH CENTURY

	1900	1910	1920	1930	1940	1950	1960	1970
POPULATION—millions	76	92	105	122	131	150	178	203
% URBAN LIVING	—	46	51	56	57	60	70	74
BIRTH RATE—No./100,000	—	30	28	21	19	24	24	18
DEATH RATE—No./100,000	17	15	13	11	11	10	10	10
DIVORCE RATE—No./100,000	—	1	2	2	2	3	2	4
IMMIGRATION—No./100,000	10	6	4	.4	.7	1.5	1.7	1.8
HIGH SCHOOL GRADS % OVER 17	6	—	17	—	51	59	65	77
COLLEGE GRADS—No./1,000	27	—	49	—	187	432	392	1,133
LIFE EXPECTANCY—years at birth	—	—	54	60	63	68	70	70
% OVER 21 VOTING FOR PRESIDENT	—	—	41	—	58	—	60	—
GROSS NATIONAL PRODUCT $ BILLION	—	—	—	103	100	285	504	977
GOV'T EXPENDITURE $ BILLION	—	—	—	9	14	74	137	220

(From the U.S. Census Bureau's "Statistical Abstracts"—1972)

The twenties in the U.S. might be looked upon as a great celebration for the victorious wartime crusade. Not only were the might of Germany, the greed of the Kaiser, and the nationalistic power struggles of Europe laid to rest by the superior moral and material resources of the U.S., but also the vaunted superiority of European culture was shown up as weak and ineffective in the face of America's youthful vigor and purity. Technology, too, was seen as an eminently American invention and asset that had demonstrated its superiority over the aristocratic traditions of Europe. This, in turn, was seen as a final vindication of the American way—of democracy, free enterprise, and pragmatic problem-solving.

The opportunities for designing new patterns of living were created by a combination of novel assets, available to nearly every American family, which only a generation before were only remotely available to the wealthy. The incorporation of the automobile into the pattern was an essential ingredient and one that had numerous unforeseen consequences. Buying cars on credit, for instance, suddenly became a universal practice and was rapidly extended to other commodities, thus altering the entire economy. The mobility that the automobile made possible was accompanied by the growth of a major mass entertainment and leisure-time industry that provided places to visit, and the workingman's work week was shortened in rapid stages from seventy-two hours per week to forty, providing the time needed to travel. For the first time, people came to expect, then get, annual vacations that served the same ends. Internal migration was greatly facilitated, to the point where moving from one part of the country to another became a fashion, an adventure, with little of the risk and uncertainty previously associated with it. The "melting pot" characteristics of the American population thus accelerated and had the effect of diminishing the regional and nationalistic traits of population groups. In the process, of course, local community influences on the individual diminished, family ties loosened, and the pressure of public opinion was attenuated.

From today's vantage point, the behavior of the people during the prohibition era appears adolescent—pleasure seeking, reckless, irresponsible, and short-sighted. This stage of development of the American culture might be looked upon as the transitional one between a pattern in which tradition served as a model of behavior and one in

WAYWARD YOUTH IN THE 1920s

"The low-cut gown, the rolled hose and short skirts are born of the Devil and are carrying the present and future generations to chaos and destruction."

Quote by President Murphy of the University of Florida, in Frederick Lewis Allen, Only Yesterday *(New York: Perennial Library, 1931).*

which the individual independently designed his own style of life and standards of conduct. As a transition, the freedom from old restraints, and the abuse of this freedom, seemed more conspicuous than did the examples of independent, mature decision-making.

DRINKING PATTERNS

Highlighting the mood of the times were the new patterns of drinking that appeared. The atmosphere of

illegality in which drinking took place, and the absence of
any great sense of guilt over its illegality, set the tone. The
selection process that screened into the drinking fraternity
those in defiance of the Anti-Saloon League and the WCTU
created a common bond. This cult-like character of drinking is found today in the marihuana cult (but not among
the hard drug users), and for similar reasons. The bond
was of a type that arises when groups find themselves in
the same boat together for a common purpose and against
a common enemy.

One of the most dramatic changes that occurred was the
abrupt incorporation of women into the drink culture on an
equal basis with men, and the extension of the practices to
younger groups. The saloon with its dominant masculine
theme was replaced by the cocktail party and the speakeasy, where women were equal in numbers to men. Women's
liberation extended far beyond this practice, and into areas
previously confined to women of lower levels of respectability. Smoking cigarettes became another national habit
that originated during World War I, and was supported by
women as well as men. Women's clothing fashions, hair-
styles, and use of cosmetics changed so markedly that new
major industries were generated to meet the demand. The
model for female attractiveness became the object of imita-
tion by nearly all women, young and old, and was epitomized by the very visible examples seen in the movies. Thus
was launched the almost universal self-consciousness concerning feminine appearance which has characterized
American women ever since, heavily supported by the advertising world and to the immense profit of enterprising
merchants.

The cocktail party was invented in the early twenties
and has since become a standard ingredient of the culture.
Sometimes, the fortuitous acquisition of a supply of liquor
by someone supplied the excuse for a party. Thus, offering

EARLY BIRTH CONTROL AGITATION

Revelations of the existence of a quietly functioning "birth control clinic" at Fifth Avenue (Manhattan) combined with agitation over a clinic in Chicago have again placed in the foreground of public attention one of the most vexing and important of medico-social problems.

Opponents of birth control base their objections chiefly on the danger of widespread immorality if contraceptive information is freely available. The fear of pregnancy they believe to be the most effective check to promiscuity with the majority of people. There is likely to be a clash over the subject in the 68th Congress.

From Time *magazine's summary of news in 1923.*

liquor to friends became a standard token of hospitality, and the most impressive show of hospitality was the offer of pure Scotch (allegedly) smuggled from abroad. More often, however, the cocktail party started with a supply of more or less purified denatured alcohol that was made into gin to serve in various mixed-drink concoctions. "Bathtub" gin referred to the place where the mixing sometimes was done. Drinking while driving cars was a more dangerous invention of the times. On college campuses, drinking at football games became nearly universal, a tradition still in existence, and still accompanied by the atmosphere of carefree abandonment that typified the twenties.

The bootlegger became a new social fixture, to the point where few areas of the country of any size were without his services. Each college campus had its own bootlegger, every hotel had one on call to make deliveries, on many street corners they did their business out of multi-pocket-lined coats. Even the nation's capital had its bootleggers.

YOUTH

Adolescent assertiveness and rebellion, accompanied by the increasing freedom of expression permitted women, placed another major part of the population in the forefront of change. Most of the derogatory observations made today about the youth culture are merely repetitions of what happened during the twenties. The irresponsible and reckless tendencies of adolescents were sharply and

JOHN STUART MILL "ON LIBERTY" (1858)

"Such questions involve considerations of liberty, only in so far as leaving people to themselves is always better than controlling them . . . there are questions relating to interference with trade which are essentially questions of liberty: such as the Maine Law, the prohibition of importation of opium into China . . . all cases, in short, where the object of the interference is to make it impossible or difficult to obtain a particular commodity. These interferences are objectionable, not as infringements on the liberty of the producer or seller, but on that of the buyer."

dramatically enhanced by the mobility supplied by the automobile, the intoxication by rotten bootleg liquor, and the rapidly developing sense of sexual freedom experienced

by women. The rapid adoption of birth control measures
served as a handy device to reinforce adolescent pleasure
seeking and defiance of tradition. The radio, the phono-
graph, and the motion picture offered a new array of pleasurable options, appealing chiefly to youth, and a new brand
of folk music and dancing rapidly evolved. The fancy
speakeasies soon became expensive nightclubs where entertainment assumed new characteristics unhampered by the
old Victorian morality. Mass entertainment began its evolution into the major industry it is today. An important by-
product of this series of events was its contribution to very
fundamental American motives. Suddenly, there became
available to all people an exciting list of pleasurable activities, coupled with the mobility and the increased leisure
time needed to take advantage of them. To exploit them
fully, a certain amount of career ambition was required to
come up with the necessary financing. Thus, the growing
industrialization of the country, with its advancing technology, found no difficulty recruiting the people needed to
man its machines. An obstacle to industrialization in other
countries frequently arises in ways not recognized but related to this phenomenon. The incentives used to recruit
and train industrial manpower are the prospects of acquiring products and services that can be bought with wages
earned. If these inducements are not available, or not attractive, then little incentive remains to enlist the population in the industrialization of a country. These assets,
however, were sharply brought to bear in the American
economy. Perhaps most important of all was the fact that
American industry early saw its consumers as being its own
workers, so that enhancing the consumer's prosperity,
which is always desired by industry, was recognized as
consistent with enhancing the workers' lot. Other nations
which have sought to industrialize have, instead, seen their

consumers as the people of other nations rather than their own workers, and so have not provided the incentives needed to improve worker productivity. Workers need something they regard as worth working for in order to acquire the incentives to learn occupational skills. As the new American culture matured, somewhat sounder objectives came to the fore, such as owning one's own home, and sending children to college. During the twenties, going to college greatly increased in popularity, but not universally for the purpose of improving the education of children. The college campus had quickly become known as a haven of freedom from both family restraint and the responsibility of adult life. This served to attract many young people who may or may not have also accidently acquired some sort of education.

The great adventure of youth was indoctrination into the drinking society, in a way that is now being repeated with drug usage. The president of Carnegie Tech in 1925, complained that the Pittsburgh director of prohibition was trying to enlist college students as informers, to spy on one another and to identify bootleggers. At M.I.T. in 1926, it was reported that each fraternity had its own bootlegger who made a call once each week to take orders for the weekend drinking that took place. Dr. Nicholas Murray Butler, President of Columbia, reported "the disregard of law and contempt for laws have greatly increased and are still increasing." Dr. Charles Eliot, President of Harvard, as early as 1920 said that "the so-called best people of the country are causing trouble in all parts of the country— teaching lawlessness to the young men who are going to be the leaders of the future."

THE NEW MORALITY

The growing contempt for prohibition enforcement efforts was intensified by numerous shadowy stories, not unlike those arising in wartime. These stories pictured the enforcement agents and courts as corrupt, capable of inhuman and unconstitutional practices, but generally easy to outwit. The standard symbol of masculinity among both young and old tended to become the courage and cleverness one exhibited in finding loopholes in the legal system. As the prohibition era advanced through the twenties, the growing evidence of organized crime and gang wars helped spread the legend of police and court incompetence. Some of the gangster leaders were actually looked upon as Robin Hoods, serving the interests of the common man in conflict with a corrupt system.

In spite of the general disregard for the prohibition laws and the many signs of social harm done by them, obviously outweighing from the beginning any good that might have come from them, there was little sentiment abroad for repeal until the end of the decade. In retrospect, it seems that the laws served the interests of both the wets and the drys, in spite of the fact that they were not enforced, and a lesson concerning the present drug problem might be read into this. The drys, for instance, seemed to feel quite vindicated in their noble cause by having labeled the sale and manufacture of liquor as illegal. Thereby, they identified by constitutional amendment those who continued to use alcohol, or traffic in it, as inferior citizens. Undoubtedly, the major share of dry support came from smalltown, rural, mostly Midwest, Protestant, Anglo-Saxon stock. The "inferiors" were the big-city dwellers who were mostly Catholic and southern European in ancestry. This neat categorization served the soul-satisfying purpose of establishing who

were the "good" and the "bad" Americans, and apparently
this is all that was desired. The wets, on the other hand,
although labeled as something less than "good Americans,"
felt compensated by the pleasure that flowed from their
practices. It also became increasingly evident that defiance
of the law had become an essential ingredient of such practices. Largely, perhaps, because of a general sense of confidence that the individual was relatively free from punishment
in spite of his defiance, the defiance itself acquired a
mystique that had its own desirable values. In other words,
it apparently appeared to many that legalization of drinking
would serve to take away much of its fun. Later, gang kill-
ings and victims of poisoned booze were disillusioning, however, and as their toll accumulated a more sober view of
prohibition began to prevail.

It is no accident that some of the literary leaders of the
times also became famous for their exposure of Victorian
hypocrisy and their advocacy of free-love, easy-living, and
unrestricted drinking. Sinclair Lewis, H. L. Mencken, F.
Scott Fitzgerald, and Eugene O'Neill were examples. For
the common man and woman, it became the gossip colum-
nist and the *True Story* scandal magazine that served as
spokesmen. Old fashioned morality and standards had
clearly lost their excitement in favor of the new.

In any period of major transition in society, a retrospec-
tive view tends to emphasize the new trends that are
emerging instead of the old ones that are waning, even
though the latter might actually be more prevalent. It must
not be forgotten that, in spite of the changes in society and
in social values that were occurring, the old ways still had
their place and their power. The old-fashioned proponents
of a puritanical way of life, based on hard work and post-
ponement of pleasure, were less vocal and less newsworthy,
but still numerous. When the Great Depression settled its

oppressive disillusionment on the country in the thirties, middle America could feel somewhat vindicated by blaming it on the recklessness and speculative fervor of the twenties, while the supporters of the newer viewpoint could blame it on prohibition and conservative Republicanism. In any event, those who survived the depression were the ones who learned to foresake pleasure in favor of self-denial and hard work. It might be considered an index of the importance and influence of the older American way by examining what remains of it today. Islands of it still survive in parts of New England and the South, and where it survives it tends to be in those communities having small turnovers of population in which public opinion still has a significant influence over individual conduct. Those people who are born into these communities and find these forces unacceptable tend to leave for other parts of the country, leaving the traditional viewpoint essentially unchallenged. Rebellious youth does not stay to fight the system but tends to go elsewhere to join forces with stronger allies.

CHILD-REARING

Child-rearing practices are striking manifestations of cultural patterns, and this area of American life became enveloped in the sweeping changes that were occurring. The old standard against which new experiments were contrasted was one in which children were once valued for the work they could contribute to the family's farming, and for this function obedience to parental control and following the parental model were esteemed. During the twenties, a variety of new fashions swept the country, including new theories and practices in education having, at least, the over-all effect of making childhood a legitimate subject to study. Children acquired a new importance in society and in the family, to the extent that an increasing amount of the total decision-making in both areas included a consideration for children. The increasing emphasis on children was especially evident to Europeans then and now who, when they observe the American family, are often struck by the central importance attached to them. It would be incorrect to say that any particularly new style of raising children developed, but it would be correct to say that the question of how to do it was no longer taken for granted by parents. Sometimes it is alleged that this period was one in which a new permissiveness pervaded child care and public education, the "progressive education" concepts of John Dewey. At least, progressive education received a great deal of attention as one of the possible methods, thus placing the more coercive approach on the defensive. Once the American family moved off the farm and out of the traditional crafts, children ceased having an economic value measured in numbers. Instead, they began to have a new value—namely, as a route through which a family's upward strivings could be satisfied through the successes of the children. Emphasis on concentrating resources on a few who might do well in moving up the establishment's ladder of success rather than on many who might supply manpower for the farm entered the picture. As a result, families became smaller, small enough, perhaps, to fit into a Model T. Birth control sophistication made family planning feasible and acceptable. No longer was having children a traditional obligation or an accident of marriage. Instead, it became an option to accept, reject, or postpone. Having a child for emotional fulfillment, especially for the mother, became one of the incentives now available. These new trends not only improved the conditions of living for children, but also placed greater demands, more complex expectations, on children. A family's reputation in the community often rested on what its children did, more than on what the parents did.

THE GOVERNMENT AND WALL STREET

A discussion of the cultural patterns of the prohibition era should not overlook the role of the federal government and Wall Street. Harding's administration was clouded by a mysterious scandal over the Teapot Dome incident, the facts of which were never made clear to the public, but in the midst of which Harding himself mysteriously died. Coolidge's administration served as a model of mediocrity in all things, which though not tainted with scandals of the Harding type, never attracted more than passing interest from the public. Hoover presided over the stock market panic of 1929 and the resulting onset of a depression. The over-all effect of the response of the elected leadership of the nation to these events was to convince the new culture that no leadership was needed, for, indeed, little direction was forthcoming from the top. The late twenties were highlighted much more vividly by what was going on in Wall Street. A wild and reckless speculative boom developed that seemed markedly in keeping with the general trend toward national irresponsible euphoria. Fortunes were made on all hands, and vast numbers of people began to gamble on the market. When the market collapsed in November, 1929, savings and credit were wiped out on all sides. Although a number of credible economic theories can be found to explain the depression that followed, few efforts have been made to see it as largely a psychological depression. Evidence that the harsh period between late 1929 and 1934 was largely the result of a general psychological rather than primarily an economic depression is shown by the reversal that took place psychologically, then economically, under the New Deal. Disappointment, disillusionment, re-placement of optimistic faith with profound confusion and a reaction in the direction of extreme conservatism played a very considerable, perhaps major, role. The long period of the depression provided the luxury of time with nothing to do except to pessimistically re-examine the styles and values that developed during the twenties. Democracy and capital-ism were questioned seriously, technology was placed on the list of suspected evils, prohibition was clearly seen as a failure, Wall Street was depicted as the exploiter of the masses, and a leaderless government as less than a blessing. The country wanted a new crusade in which they could team their efforts to re-build the nation, and for this job a new leader was needed. Roosevelt and the New Deal filled the requirements sufficiently well to reverse the downward spiral of the economy, and the dwindling faith in the system.

Chapter

4

THE GROWTH OF ORGANIZED CRIME

CAUSES AND RESULTS

Organized crime became an integral part of the American scene during the prohibition era and was made possible because of the conditions that prohibition created, conditions that are necessary for organizing a nation-wide network of underworld enterprises. These conditions included:

1. A large demand for goods or services that was prevented from being met through legal channels by restrictive legislation.

2. A substantial reservoir of money to purchase these goods or services, and a general willingness to pay prices high enough to make large profits possible.

3. Some framework of organization, having clear-cut objectives and means of achieving them and staffed by people prepared to work toward a common end, stooping to any means, the end being the preservation of the organization for the purpose of effectively and efficiently

achieving the objectives. This skeletal organization was the Mafia membership, which had already an established code, a system of communication, and strategically placed representatives.

4. A system prevailing among politicians, police, and courts that was prepared to overlook the activities of the organization, and ethically prepared to share in the profits.

5. A sufficient degree of public acceptance of those persons who flouted the restrictive laws to inhibit the development of influential counter-movements.

All these conditions existed during the twenties, and organized crime did, indeed, take advantage of them. There also existed a major deterrent to success, which made the organizational efforts difficult and violently disruptive. This deterrent was inherent in the fact that the potential leaders of the organization were unprepared to employ democratic methods of choosing a hierarchy, since each aspired to the positions of power; and in the struggles for power that ensued, much blood was spilled. A time-honored business concept, however, served to bring about ultimate success, and this was the realization of those concerned that through organized, collective efforts, a monopoly of the potential trade was possible—monopoly offering the opportunities for market control that could then sustain the organization.

As early as 1920, an enterprising underworld figure— Johnny Torrio of Chicago—foresaw the lucrative possibilities of large-scale bootlegging in which manufacture, distribution, and retailing were all under centralized control. He also quickly found that there were many competitors for the available business, some mere amateurs, but others more worthy of his attention. By liquidating some in a business-like way, others in less business-like ways, and by consolidating his operations with still others, he rather quickly organized a very sizable operation. He employed a gang of thugs to both intimidate his competitors and to induce speakeasies to buy his products. As his organization grew in size, he sought a suitable lieutenant to assist him, and found one in a twenty-three-year-old Sicilian named Al Capone who was currently passing himself off as a second-hand furniture dealer. Torrio retired peacefully soon afterward and moved to New York City, leaving Capone to run the organization.

The Chicago organization was correct in its prediction that success in achieving a local monopoly would become very profitable, but they did not anticipate another consequence—namely, that others recognized the profits to be made and sought to move in on them. Hence, the long series of Chicago gang wars.

By 1923, Capone had 300 men working for him, and then began to concentrate on the task of pacifying the police and politicians. He made his headquarters in Cicero, a suburb of Chicago, and had his own man elected as mayor. He entered the retail, as well as the wholesale, end of the bootlegging business and soon had a chain of 161 of his own speakeasies, while selling to about 10,000 others. One of his competitors who posed a particularly serious threat was a florist named O'Banion who had a bootlegging business on the side. The problem was finally resolved by murdering O'Banion. Typically, however, Capone provided him with an elaborate funeral, including a $10,000 casket and twenty-six truckloads of flowers. None of the Capone mob participating in the murder was ever apprehended.

In ten years, at least 500 gang murders took place in Chicago alone. Few of these murders led to arrests, and each one more strongly entrenched the position of the Capone organization. In 1927, federal agents estimated that Capone was getting $60,000,000 annually in revenue from liquor alone. In addition, he had gambling operations gross-

PUBLIC SERVICE FUNCTION OF
ORGANIZED CRIME

(Press conference with Al Capone on the occasion of his leaving Chicago for Florida) "I'm going to St. Petersburg, Fla. tomorrow. Let the worthy citizens of Chicago get their liquor the best they can. I'm sick of the job—it's a thankless one and full of grief.

"I'm spending the best years of my life as a public benefactor. I've given people the light pleasures—shown them a good time—all I get is abuse. Public service is my motto. But I'm not appreciated. My wife and mother hear so much about what a terrible criminal I am, it's getting too much for them, and I'm just sick of it all myself. I wish all my friends and enemies a Merry Christmas . . . That's all they'll get from me this year."

From Time *magazine's summary of news in 1927.*

ing $25,000,000, and $10,000,000 came from other rackets. The rackets were usually various schemes designed to sell "protection," first to merchants, and later to ensure employers against labor trouble. Failure to buy protection typically resulted in a merchant's store being dynamited. Between 1927 and 1929, there were 157 reported bombings in Chicago, apparently connected with these activities.

The automobile was a prime tool of the gangsters, not only as a mode of cargo transport, but as a target for highjacking, as mobile fortresses, and for quick getaways.

Capone became a kind of folk hero in many circles. He insisted that newspapers regard him as a businessman engaged in the business of hospitality. He received fan letters from all over the world, and he became so widely known that his name became a household word everywhere. He contributed $260,000 to elect "Big Bill" Thompson mayor of Chicago, and when elected, Thompson stated that the "crime wave" in Chicago was "just newspaper talk."

So much discredit was being leveled at the state of Illinois because of the gang activities in Chicago that a liquor control law was finally passed. It was so thoroughly amended by the time it was passed, however, that it was ineffective. It provided for licenses to sell liquor (although forbidden in the federal law), and 9,000 were sold. The licensed dealer became, then, immune to interference from state officials. The local and state police, therefore, participated insignificantly in the enforcement of the liquor laws, and the federal government had a total of only 134 agents to cover the entire state.

Capone was finally arrested in 1931 for income tax evasion and died almost immediately after release from a federal prison eleven years later.

The Mafia was a Sicilian import with a long tradition of serving members' interests at the expense of the establishment. During the 1920s, it existed in the U.S. only as small, local "families" without a national organization. The various families, however, successively moved into the bootlegging and speakeasy business, mostly in the big cities, and promptly found themselves competing against one another. The gang wars in Chicago were repeated in New York, and to a lesser extent in other big cities, and as the prohibition era moved toward the thirties, it became evident that the principal rivals in these wars were the different Mafia families. An especially bloody series of assassinations finally prompted Salvatore Marazano, in New York City in 1930, to arrange a "peace treaty." To achieve some unanim-

ORIGINS OF THE ILLEGAL TRAFFIC IN NARCOTICS

Prior to the passing of the Harrison Narcotic Act in 1914, opium and its derivatives were easily and cheaply obtainable from all drug stores. The passage of the act, requiring that all narcotics be dispensed solely through doctors' prescriptions, suddenly unleashed several hundred thousand addicts in an onslaught on doctors for prescriptions, far more than could be handled in anything approaching a clinically responsible manner. A Supreme Court decision in 1919 (*Webb* vs. *the U.S.*) declared it illegal for a physician to prescribe for a known addict, and numerous arrests and convictions of physicians followed. An attempt was made to cope with the problem by setting up a total of forty clinics in as many cities between 1918 and 1921. During this period, the clinics operated much the same as the present "British System" does, and served to bring the problem under some semblance of control. However, the government (via the Treasury Department) abruptly closed these clinics in 1921, throwing the unmet demands of the addicts into the waiting arms of drug bootleggers. Thus was launched the system of illegal narcotic traffic, which has profitably flourished ever since. It is interesting to note that in 1921 there was already established a network of bootleggers ready to profit from the sale of illegal alcohol, a business simultaneously inaugurated with the passing of the Eighteenth Amendment.

Author's interpretation of material in first chapter of Troy Duster, The Legislation of Morality, New York: The Free Press, 1970.

ity, however, it was deemed necessary to kill off forty
men. This was the beginning of organized crime on a nation-wide basis. Lucky Luciano succeeded Maranzano by
having him murdered and set about using the organization
for large-scale racketeering. Luciano finally was arrested
and deported to Italy in 1936, largely through the efforts of
New York District Attorney Thomas E. Dewey. It was
widely believed at the time that Luciano's removal effectively broke up the organization. Instead, Frank Costello
took over control, following another series of power maneuvers, and succeeded, finally, in bringing about a fairly
durable peace within the ranks.

The Mafia consists of separate "families," each with its
chief and council, but all organized into a national commission. The national leadership serves mostly to replace
leaders, settle inter-family disputes, and maintain harmony.
Actual business operations and policy are determined at
the local level, and each family engages in its own particular
set of enterprises. Only a couple of the families, for instance,
appear to have entered the narcotics business. It is estimated
that nation-wide there are a total of twenty-four families with
5,000 to 6,000 members, of which 2,000 are in New York City
and its environs, and comprise 5 families. The other centers
appear to be Boston, Rhode Island, Chicago, New Orleans,
Detroit, Cleveland, Tampa, and Los Angeles-San Diego.
Cities such as Las Vegas and Miami seem to be free-trade
areas in which several families operate without anyone
having staked out a territory. Territorial boundaries appear
to be determined by monopolies over certain enterprises,
rather than geographic, so that there exists some overlap-
ping geographically.

With the repeal of prohibition in 1934, the organization
leaders appreciated the necessity of finding new kinds of
businesses. Not only did they have large amounts of capi-

tal to invest, but they also had a sizable manpower pool that could cause them untold trouble if its members ended up unemployed. The businesses they were most familiar with were prostitution and gambling, and there was a growing number of legal openings for gambling in Nevada, Cuba, and the Bahamas. Labor racketeering had been experimented with to some extent, and became one of the more major post-prohibition enterprises. Legitimate businesses such as hotels and trucking lines also offered diverse opportunities for branching out and were infiltrated quite heavily. The Mafia control of waterfront workers' unions and trucking lines which served the docks of New York provided some of the New York groups with the assets needed to develop a flourishing narcotics trade, capitalizing as well on their connections in the Mediterranean region where the supplies came from.

The story of the unification of the underworld unfolds much like the transition from feudalism to nationalism in Europe. Local, powerful barons could see some advantages in forming collective groups for the common defense, but were unwilling to give up any of their own authority, and were not prepared to have the leadership fall to anyone other than themselves. Thus, the baronial wars resulted in a long struggle for power, sustained by the realization that the common objective was desirable. Torrio in Chicago was one of the first, or perhaps the first, local Mafia baron to acquire power and to see the virtues in a broad organization. It took many years of bloody rivalry, however, before leaders appeared who placed the survival of the organization above their own power interests, and thus achieved a modicum of peace. The Mafia national organization is probably still much like the early days in England under King John, when a group of barons could depose a king anytime they considered it desirable. The national organization, then serves mostly for the common defense of the local units; the locals are the operating units.

An economic view of history, although still imperfect, comes closer than most other interpretations to providing us with credible theories of past events. According to this view, the viability of any social institution ultimately rests on its economic value to the culture that supports it. Organized crime has proven itself to be viable, a durable fixture of the culture. It might be profitable to enumerate some of the economic values it maintains that ensure its viability.

ECONOMIC BENEFITS OF ORGANIZED CRIME

1. Organized crime provides merchandise and/or services to satisfy pleasurable (rather than necessary) needs of people denied them through legal channels. Examples of these include alcoholic beverages in times and places where they are prohibited by law or excessively costly because of taxation; gambling; prostitution; drugs; and blackmarkets in consumer products during periods of scarcity.

2. It provides supplementary income to underpaid public servants such as the police and local inspectors.

3. It provides campaign money for politicians running for office, a particular windfall for relatively unknown campaigners who have no other sources of contributions.

4. It sometimes provides a substitute police protection to merchants through its control over people capable of doing damage.

5. It provides loans for high-risk enterprises that could not be financed through banks and other loan agencies.

THE CURRENT ROLE OF THE F.B.I. IN ORGANIZED CRIME INVESTIGATION

"The FBI has plenty of agents to search for stolen cars, infiltrate anti-war rallies, keep files on congressmen and polish J. Edgar Hoover's image. But it has assigned only four to the Justice Department's vital 17-city drive against the Mafia.

The campaign against the centipede crime syndicate is spearheaded by strike forces in each city. These are run by tough, young Justice Department lawyers, who have 228 federal agents from various law enforcement agencies working under them.

The confidential strike force rosters show how badly the FBI has let down the rest of the anti-Mafia team. Only four of the 228 federal agents come from the FBI. The rest are Treasury, narcotics, postal and securities agencies.

Footnote: Drug addicts, who must steal to feed their habit, have caused the alarming increase in unorganized crime. And the Mafia is the brains behind most organized crime. Yet the nation's foremost law enforcement agency, the 7,800-man FBI, turned down President Lyndon Johnson's appeal to help crack down on the illicit drug traffic and provides only marginal help in the drive against the Mafia."

From Jack Andersons syndicated newspaper column, September 3, 1971.

6. It reduces the cost to consumers of certain merchandise whose price has been raised steeply through taxation (e.g., cigarettes in New York at present).

7. It provides for investment purposes, ways of accumulating capital that are unidentifiable to the government.

8. It provides leisure-time activities and entertainment in areas otherwise bereft of these advantages because of various legal constraints, thus contributing to the tourist-attracting qualities of an area.

9. It provides jobs for ex-convicts who ordinarily find it difficult to obtain employment.

Thus, the goods and services in which organized crime deals constitute a business enterprise supported mainly by large segments of the general, law-abiding population. It invariably exists and thrives only with the protection of local police, courts, and politicians. In areas of the population where respect for legal institutions and processes is low, support for the businesses engaged in by organized crime is high, and vice versa. By virtue of the very support these enterprises get from the public, the public itself is thereby sharing in the corruption, a phenomenon that tends to perpetuate the system. A mutual dependency tends to lead to mutual co-existence, a lesson that nations might learn from one another.

The President's Crime Commission reported in 1967 that only twelve cities of the country had special investigation units assigned to organized crime, and only six had special prosecution units. Nevertheless, the Commission estimated that organized crime was a dominant influence in at least twenty-five large cities, although not recognized in this light. The Federal Bureau of Investigation and the Department of Justice would appear to be the logical agencies to deal with the problem since they are both interstate and international in scope. They, however, have paid very little attention to it, only a fraction of the attention, for instance, that they have paid to the highly dubious threat of communist infiltration. When Robert Kennedy became Attorney General, he found that 400 FBI agents were assigned to the New York City area to investigate communism (and found little to make their efforts pay), but only four to investigate the Mafia. Kennedy's statements about the situation, and his apparent determination to neutralize the FBI Director's domination of the Bureau, indicated that a change in federal policy would be forthcoming. There is little to suggest, however, that this happened. When Ramsay Clark became Attorney General, there was, again, hope for a new orientation supported by Clark's evident awareness of the problem and his lack of sympathy with the FBI Director. These hopes, too, seem to have been frustrated. John Mitchell, who succeeded Clark, repeatedly took strong stands endorsing strict enforcement of the laws, but he was completely in sympathy with the FBI Director and had no apparent interest in focusing on the organized crime issue.

The actual crimes generally committed by the organization are local and state violations, and calculatedly so, for it is in this area of enforcement where their influence is greatest and protection most assured. There are relatively few federal laws involved, although the income tax evasion laws always represent a logical route through which to attack the organization, as was done with Capone. Interstate traffic in stolen cars, interstate flight to escape prosecution, carrying concealed weapons across state borders, violations of the feeble gambling tax law, and interstate traffic concerned with prostitution are other areas of possible federal involvement. Only minor pressure has been exerted for new laws specifically designed to give the Justice Department a logical focus of attack. A set of laws not yet applied, but striking at the heart of the problem, would be the anti-trust laws, and the business-like nature of organized crime makes this approach unusually appropriate.

From what can be learned from other histories, it would seem reasonable to conclude that the FBI's indifference to the problem was evidence of corruption, and this might, in fact, be the case. More likely is the possibility that the problem is ignored in order to *avoid* corruption, a kind of reverse blackmail, or corruption by default. In any event, as was the case with enforcement of the prohibition laws, there has never arisen in the country any great hue and cry to purge ourselves of organized crime. Therefore, it continues quietly to do business and make huge profits.

Chapter
5

THE DRINKING CULTURE
AND DRINKING PATTERNS

A<small>LL</small> that is necessary to manufacture alcohol is to permit a sweetened liquid, such as berry juice, to stand in a container in a warm place for a few days. Consequently, nearly all cultures have early discovered the virtues of alcoholic beverages almost simultaneously with their development of simple containers that could hold liquids. The remarkable, almost universal phenomenon is that each culture that made these discoveries also found such pleasures in sampling the results that there developed the abuse of alcoholic beverages. When questions are raised about why people sometimes may drink excessively, the answer is simply found in the universality of the pleasure-producing consequences, coupled with the simple realization that pleasure usually is the motivating force behind many, many human behaviors, rational and otherwise. The issue of the problem drinker is as universal as the practice of fermenting fruit juice. Nearly all cultures have encountered the problem in significant, and often alarming, measure, and almost as many have failed to find satisfactory solutions. The alcoholic exhibits a personality that distinguishes him from those people in a culture who behave in a consistently rational and responsible fashion, but not from those who typically exhibit other forms of less than responsible behavior. Problem drinking, then, is likely to co-exist with other problems, and much can be learned from understanding the common denominators that these problems share.

THE CLASSICAL ERA

The Greeks, during their 500 years or so of rather advanced civilization before the Christian era, often recorded their thoughts about the scope of their alcohol problems, and were particularly prone to emphasize the differences in drinking patterns among the different sub-cultures in Greece. Perhaps they too, as we do today, em-

PREDICTIONS ON THE FATE OF SALOONS

QUOTES FROM VARIOUS CONTEMPORARY NEWS ACCOUNTS

"The temptation to the lazy, prompted by distillers and brewers lending credit, forces upon the community saloons everywhere, because even in a hole in a wall a considerable daily income can be earned. The political machine of liquor dealers wields, through the ubiquitous saloons, a vicious influence over voters."

Former President Taft's observation on saloons, 1919.

"The policy of the government will be to see that the social and political evils that have existed in the pre-Prohibition era shall not be revived nor permitted again to exist. Failure to do this honestly and courageously will be a living reproach to us all.

I ask especially that no state shall by law or otherwise authorize the return of the saloon either in its old form or in some modern guise."

President Roosevelt on the matter of repeal, 1934.

Governor Al Smith of New York: "I will never aprove any law which, directly or indirectly, permits the return of the saloon."

Senator Copeland of New York: "Under no circumstances must the baneful evils of the corner saloon come back to haunt us."

Senator Tydings of Maryland: "I am ready to fight against its return with every bit of energy at my command."

Mr. Anderson of the Wickersham Commission: "The saloon is as completely a thing of the past as human slavery."

Congressman Oliver of New York: "Hereafter no saloon shall be maintained anywhere in the U.S. under the penalty of two years in jail."

On the return of saloons by advocates of repeal.

phasized unfairly how people other than themselves tended to drink excessively. In other words, few if any cultures have taken any national pride in drunkenness, but each has tended to ascribe more excesses to others than to themselves.

The Athenians were often described, especially by other Greeks, as heavy drinkers, in spite of the fact that there generally existed strong social pressures against excessive drinking. The Spartans, on the other hand, enjoyed a reputation for being more moderate in their drinking habits, in keeping with their tradition of espousing moderation in all things. Alexander the Great was, apparently, a serious alcoholic who died during a drinking bout.

The drinking habits of the Romans during the early days of building the Empire tended to be confined to ceremonial occasions, but as prosperity and high living crept into the later Empire, drinking, along with other similar practices, tended to assume new proportions. Alongside the general moral decadence that increasingly prevailed, excessive drinking became rampant, invaded the workday of the bureaucracy, and became uncharacteristically common even among the statesmen of the day. Nevertheless, the sober statesman commanded the greater respect, and prohibitions against women drinking continued to remain in force. Women who violated these restrictions did so at the expense of massive public disapproval. In general, excessive

IN DEFENSE OF PROHIBITION

"In spite of the successful efforts which have been made to wreck it, Prohibition has not been a failure as its enemies claim. . . . Moreover, I am . . . convinced that the violation of the Eighteenth Amendment and the racketeering in liquor were both deliberately encouraged by the controlling Federal authorities, and by many minor authorities."

Address by Governor Gifford Pinchot, of Pennsylvania, in 1933.

". . . in another generation I believe that liquor will have disappeared not only from our politics but from our memories. . . . There is a demand for every living being in the United States to respect and abide by the laws of the Republic. Let men who are rending the moral fibre of the Republic through easy contempt of the Prohibition Law . . . remember that they set up an example and breed contempt for law which will ultimately destroy the Republic."

Address to Congress by President Harding in 1922.

"I am in entire accord with the conclusions that enforcement of the National Prohibition Act made a bad start which has affected enforcement ever since. . . . I unite with my colleagues, nevertheless, in agreement that the Eighteenth Amendment must not be repealed, and differing from some of them, I have been forced to conclude that a further trial should be made of the enforcibility of the Eighteenth Amendment under the present organization and with the help of the recommended improvements."

Statement by George Wickersham, Chairman of the "Wickersham" Commission appointed by President Hoover to investigate the enforcement problem in 1931.

drinking patterns appeared to have developed alongside a general hardening of social institutions, as it does in our culture today, changing, therefore, from a set of convivial acts to more rebellious ones. Similar changes appear to have been characteristic of American drinking patterns as the nation, too, changed from a growing, frontier-oriented society to a more institutionalized and prosperous one. The change, in other words, was not so much a change in the amount of alcohol consumed, but in the circumstances under which it was consumed.

The invading Gauls from the north were often cited by Roman historians as prone to celebrate their victories with drunken orgies. More than once, the Roman legions took advantage of the drunkenness of their enemies by snatching victory from the mouth of defeat. Roman writers also classified many other national groups according to the reputation they had earned for their typical drinking habits. The Spanish, for instance, were known as especially moderate in their drinking, and the Iberians, although considered wealthy, were known as total abstainers. The Moors and Numidians of North Africa were also abstainers (and later when converted to Muslimism incorporated abstinence into their religion). The Ethiopians were thought to be very light drinkers, as well, but the Persians were considered very heavy drinkers and were said to have very short life spans as a result. The Egyptians seemed to drink wine freely and often, and women as well as men indulged, but excesses were apparently infrequent. It is interesting that the ancient code of Hammurabi established strict regulations over traffic in wine, but none concerning the drinking of wine.

CENTRAL AND SOUTH AMERICA

The Aztecs used wine only for ceremonial occasions and most of the drinking was done by political and religious leaders.

Today, among the Indian communities of Central and South America, drinking of homemade or commercial alcoholic beverages is generally prevalent, and some examples of drinking practices deserve special note. The Indians of Chichicastanango (Guatemala), for example, drink only on festival and market days (once each week), and the drinking is universal. Scores of people become quite drunk on market days, but this is in no way looked down upon by the others. Drunkenness is often used as an excuse for wrongdoing, and the excuse is frequently accepted.

In Chamula, Mexico, the Indians are known by visiting Americans as the most drunken of all Mexicans. Everyone seems to drink, and heavily, including children. Alcoholism has been confirmed in children ten years of age. During festivals, the entire community may become quite drunk for an entire week, some natives have been known to be continuously drunk for several months at a time. There seems to be little solitary drinking. A great deal of fighting is likely to occur during drinking bouts, but whether cause or effect, there is a remarkable scarcity of other pursuits in which people engage, suggesting that more constructive social practices have been replaced by drinking.

The Viscocinos of Peru live in an Indian community of 1,800 population. The entire community drinks, but almost solely during festival occasions. Although there is a great deal of drunkenness, it has remarkably little effect on the stability of the society. People behave about the same either drunk or sober. There is very little violence and an absence of sexual misbehavior during drinking bouts.

Among the native Indian population of Santiago, Chile, who represent the working class of the community, there is a very high incidence of alcoholism as it is known in the United States. One observer estimates that 12 percent of these natives are alcoholics. In addition, there is a great deal of drunkenness among the other men who are not true alcoholics.

THE FAR EAST

In India there are many religious prohibitions against drinking in the many different religions, particularly among the Mohammedans, the Jains, and the Vaishnaivites. In the upper social classes, drinking and drunkenness are very uncommon, but it is more frequent in the lower economic classes and among the more underprivileged religious sects. People who have recently changed from an agricultural to an industrial economy tend to show an increase in drinking. In general, observers report, drinking is less prevalent and the excesses of drinking more rare than is the case in Western Europe.

In China from ancient times drinking has been prevalent, but drunkenness has been rare. Chinese seem to be sharply divided between wets and drys, with the two groups tending to exhibit the opposite extremes in drinking patterns. Wine is likely to be regarded as a food and is highly esteemed, whereas excessive drinking is likely to coincide with excessive eating.

In Japan, drunkenness and alcoholism have rapidly become major public health problems in recent years and steps are now being taken to deal with them. Tea was introduced from China during the thirteenth or fourteenth century in an attempt to lure the people away from rice wine.

EUROPE

In Russia, drunkenness and traffic in alcoholic beverages were a source of perpetual conflict in the relationship between the state and the people for centuries. The czars sought to exploit, rather than control, the drinking tendencies of the population by taxing alcoholic beverages. The people, on the other hand, tended to use alcohol as a weapon of defiance against the state by illegally manu-

facturing and consuming it. The history of the struggle between the people and the state during the hundred years or
so before the Revolution represents an interesting and unusual kind of relationship between government and the
governed, and might have been conducive to the spread and
perpetuation of excessive drinking. Today, it is reported
by American observers that drunkenness is very prevalent
in Russia. Adolescents are widely affected, and drunkenness seems to be associated with much of the juvenile
delinquency. It is one of the few social problems the government publicly admits. Writers, artists, and musicians have a
reputation for being heavy drinkers. Among the workers,
the ability to drink large amounts of alcohol or to squander
money for alcoholic beverages seems to be more esteemed
as a sign of masculinity than it is condemned by society.
This attitude seems to be a holdover from czarist days when
illicit drinking was looked upon as a token of courageous
defiance against tyranny. In agricultural communities, heavy
drinking is likely to characterize holidays and festivals.

In France, the consumption of alcoholic beverages and
all the commercial enterprises surrounding them represent
a very major component of the country's economy, and an
essential feature of the social structure. The average per
capita consumption of alcohol is on the order of thirty
kilos, as compared with fourteen for Italy, and nine for
Great Britain and the United States. The drinking of wines,
cider, and brandies pervades nearly all social occasions, is
standard form for most meals, and involves all age groups,
both sexes, and all social classes. Drinking is seldom frowned
upon, and temperance movements rarely gain much support. There is a general tendency on the part of nearly
all groups to claim healthful qualities for alcohol, the opposite for competing beverages such as Coca Cola, and to
deny drinking as a social problem. The Minister of Educa-

tion, as recently as 1939, advocated drinking wines as a health measure. Any attempt to introduce other beverages tends to meet with great resistance from many sources. The commercial interests engaged in the alcohol business exert great political power. The laws against the unlicensed manufacture and sale of alcohol are widely disregarded and indifferently enforced. Observers from other countries where there are stricter moral attitudes against drinking, such as the U.S. and England, invariably wonder at the amount of drinking that is done in France and tend to assume that alcoholism is also prevalent. The fact that, among the Western nations, France has the highest incidence of cirrhosis of the liver would indicate that a high frequency of alcoholism corresponds with the high per capita consumption of alcohol.

The English generally condemn excessive drinking and particularly any aggressive behavior associated with it. The temperance movement gets fairly good support. A recent spot survey indicated that 31 percent of adults in England never drink and twice as many of the abstainers are women as men. Since World War I, the number of court convictions for drunkenness has steadily fallen. The British have a reputation for being well behaved when drinking, and the reputation would appear to be deserved.

The Scandinavian countries are remarkable for the experience they have had in state control of the liquor traffic, and these control systems are indicative of the magnitude of the social problems attributable to alcoholism. Finland and Sweden, particularly, have used state control over liquor manufacture and sales as a way of reducing the problems of excessive drinking, and they appear to have been more successful than have the United States and Canada. Prohibitionists often cite the experience of these countries as desirable models to follow.

UNITED STATES AND CANADA

The heterogeneous nature of America's multiple cultures has prompted a number of studies into the varying drinking practices and the sub-groups within the larger society. For instance, it has been found that a higher percentage of Protestants in Canada are drinkers than Catholics, whereas in the United States, a higher percentage of Catholics are drinkers than Protestants. In both countries, a much higher percentage of men drink than do women, although the number of women drinkers has been increasing in recent years, whereas the proportion of men who drink remains more nearly constant.

Whether or not the incidence of alcoholism corresponds to the incidence of people who drink in a given group is a question of some importance, since it is much more feasible to identify drinkers than it is to identify the alcoholics, and data concerning the former are often used to discuss problems concerning the latter.

It is a well-recognized fact that, among Jews, the use of alcohol as a beverage is nearly universal, but the incidence of alcoholism is extremely low. The Irish, on the other hand, in both the United States and Ireland, show a high incidence of drinking as well as alcoholism. Among Italians in Italy drinking rates are high but alcoholism is low, whereas both rates are high among Italian-Americans. Among college graduates in the United States, the percentage of drinkers is high but alcoholism is low. These and other similar observations indicate that the incidence of drinking or the per capita consumption of alcohol cannot be used as a reliable index of the incidence of alcoholism.

Few worthwhile generalizations can be drawn about American attitudes and practices in respect to drinking because of the heterogeneous nature of the social structure.

The strong prohibitionist sentiment that led as early as the
1850s to the adoption of a prohibition law in Maine and to
the Eighteenth Amendment is indicative of three factors:
(1) the recognition of widespread excesses in the use of
alcohol; (2) strong moral condemnation of these excesses;
and (3) the political weakness of opponents of prohibition.
In France, on the other hand, drinking has been much
more prevalent than in the United States; abstinence is almost unknown, moral attitudes have been lenient, and the
alcohol interests are politically powerful. The use of state
control over alcohol traffic has been widely and vigorously
advocated in both the United States and Canada, with
both countries having experimented with various types of
prohibition; but the shambles of the prohibition era now
seem to have forever weakened these influences.

ALCOHOL AND THE AMERICAN
CULTURE

In America, the western frontier tradition has
tended to identify drinking with pleasure, recreation, and
hospitality, whereas the New England puritanical tradition
has regarded drinking as wasteful, a sign of weak character,
and a cause of social misbehavior. These two sets of traditions are contradictory but have one thing in common—
the general condemnation of drinking among women. On
the American scene, for example, drinking escapades on the
part of college boys are likely to be looked upon quite
tolerantly, but similar episodes among young girls are
more likely to be condemned. Whereas beer and tavern
drinking have been looked upon as working-class pastimes,
cocktail parties have been regarded as upper-class privileges. As a result, there has been a tendency for socially

ambitious people to abuse the cocktail ritual as a symbol of sophistication. The well-established, prosperous, small town in America tends to exhibit strong public attitudes against excessive drinking, whereas in middle-class metropolitan cultures, where public opinion has less influence, attitudes are likely to be more lenient and permissive. World War II saw a sharp rise in drinking, in per capita alcohol consumption, and in alcoholism. These indices appear to have fallen since, even though an increasing number of women are entering the drinking fraternity.

The skid row alcoholic appears to be a unique American phenomenon that seems to have been created by two factors that typify the American scene. On the one hand, America, unlike France, tends to banish its unproductive citizens from the privileges of respectable society, but provides for the care of these fringe citizens. The skid row character is fairly well taken care of in respect to food, shelter, and medical care, and the law is likely to be quite tolerant of any anti-social behavior on his part as long as he confines himself to his own world of alcoholic peers. To rise above the degradation of a skid row life to respectable society is likely to be regarded as an outstanding accomplishment, worth writing a book or making a movie about.

The alcoholic who more or less quietly gets along on a marginal level of adjustment and who is sufficiently productive to support himself is likely to be regarded with tolerance, and many of his anti-social transgressions may be overlooked. However, if he is responsible for supporting a family, or if any of his misdemeanors involve the lives of "respectable" people, he is likely to be ostracized. The number of alcoholic men of any type are numerous enough so that each one can usually manage to establish a relationship with a group of others. Within these groups there is little of what might be considered true friendship, but since

there is an absence of criticism toward one another, the
individual can salvage some degree of self-esteem from
the apparent acceptance of his irrational habits by his
group. It is not uncommon for members of these groups to
be represented on the local police forces, as employees of
restaurants or saloons, or as taxi drivers, and as such they
stand in strategic positions to protect the individual group
members. The structure of these groups is uniquely similar
to that often seen in Alcoholics Anonymous groups, wherein
the common bond is abstinence from drinking rather than
drinking itself, and the method of operation is that of a
mutual protective society. Whether the alcoholic seeks his
relationships in a group of alcoholics or in an AA group,
he is likely seeking protection and freedom from criticism
that help him maintain some semblance of self-esteem
and security. Although this support is effective in prevent-
ing the psychosis that might result if all support for self-
esteem were withdrawn, it also serves to perpetuate his
irresponsible mode of existence. The need to seek this kind
of relationship is a reaction against the condemnation with
which American society regards the alcoholic, an all-perva-
sive attitude that is not so common nor widespread in other
cultures. As a result, America's social system tends to draw
a rather definite and rigid line between reasonable drinking
and alcoholism. In other societies, such as in France, Ireland, Italy, Russia, and Poland, this line is not so definite,
and only the extremes of alcoholism are recognized, usually
when medical complications develop.

These factors must be kept in mind when we estimate the
prevalence of alcoholism. Even though sociologists or
physicians might often claim that the definition of alcoholism is too indefinite to permit accurate estimates of the
scope of the problem, the public at large seems to have no
trouble recognizing the "drinking man" in its midst. The

local group recognizes in its alcoholic members an insensitiveness, indifference, or defiance toward those social pressures, expressed as public opinion, which appear to keep other people in line. Accordingly, the drinking man is identified by these criteria, and not merely by the amount or frequency of his drinking. Thus, the outside observer is often less accurate than the community in recognizing the alcoholic because the outsider is not alert to the criteria used by the group in assessing loyalty or disloyalty in its members.

Among such groups as the Quakers, the Mennonites, the Seventh Day Adventists, and the Mormons, members are warned clearly that even slight drinking represents defiance of group influence and is a symptom of disloyalty. Since even minor drinking would pose an immediate threat of banishment, any experimenting with drinking is done with this risk in mind, and is therefore likely to be a serious sign of rebellion. On the other hand, there are some sub-cultures within a society in which drinking itself is not regarded as defiance, even though chronic alcoholism is condemned. This is especially true of Jewish and Cantonese groups, wherein drinking is acceptable but alcoholism is not. Aside from these sub-cultures, there exist fairly homogeneous groups based on socio-economic distinctions that have their own unique standards in respect to drinking and alcoholism. Physicians, for example, have very rigid, although almost completely unspoken, prohibitions against any form of drinking while on duty, and within this system even slight transgressions invoke the suspicion that the subject is guilty of irresponsibility. Certain types of top business executive groups, on the other hand, maintain a constant drinking ritual wherein certain occasions demand the acceptance of a fair amount of drinking. Yet drunkenness on these occasions is regarded as a sign of untrustworthiness.

Study of individual alcoholics reveals, invariably, a certain kind of social relationship that serves to perpetuate the drinking habit. Superficial observations of these relationships often lead investigators to suppose that one of the alcoholic's problems lies in the pressures his drinking companions place on him to drink. A deeper study will show, however, that the alcoholic characteristically seeks those people who do not criticize his drinking, including other alcoholics. He also manages to find ways of surrounding himself with people who help him "get away with it." The married alcoholic very frequently has found himself a wife who might nag him relentlessly about his drinking, but who seems quite content to care for him when he gets into trouble, almost as if she "drives him to drink" so that she can savor the sense of power that comes from caring for him when he is helpless. Nearly every alcoholic has found for himself one or more people who will offer him protection when his drinking gets him into trouble. These people may be bartenders, policemen, fellow drinkers, or taxi drivers. Mothers of alcoholics, like wives, are often unusually protective of a drunken son. The drunken crises are frequently characterized by elaborate and dramatic promises to reform, to re-establish old relationships, to make up for past mistakes, and the mother or wife who accepts these promises and forgives becomes a principal party in perpetuating the abnormal drinking patterns. In much the same way that our entire society takes a kind of pride in taking good care of the persons it has excommunicated (the aged, mentally ill, the criminals, the alcoholics) in order to make itself look superior, so many individual persons gratify their own self-esteem by maintaining a helpless alcoholic's dependency.

In America, the female alcoholic is a special type who deserves separate consideration. She has no skid row to gravitate to, and seldom finds more than one other female companion to drink with. Most likely, she will be a solitary drinker who drinks to achieve something rather than to avoid something. The wrath of public opinion falls much more heavily on the woman who drinks, so her drinking implies a greater degree of defiance or demands more secrecy than is the case with men. Consequently, there is much more anti-social behavior among women alcoholics than among men, since it occurs in a more socially defiant group. Women's record in this respect tends to heap added censure on female drunkenness, because of the common assumption that intoxication leads to all sorts of misbehavior. Like the male alcoholic, the female is prone to fall into and to be exploited in states of helplessness. The female drinker also develops dependent relationships that are necessary to perpetuate her drinking practices, and thereby manages to get others to condone her alcoholism to the extent that they protect her against the undesirable consequences of her drunkenness. The female alcoholic is perhaps more likely to be married than the male, for marriage to the male more often signifies increased responsibility that he seeks to avoid, whereas to the female it can more easily offer her the dependent state that she seeks. The married female alcoholic, however, is more likely to be kept hidden from public view, whereas the unmarried one is more likely to become conspicuous because of her tendency to seek dependent relationships in public. The male alcoholic seems more likely to abandon his marriage and the female to try to hold on to hers, and for the same reasons—to avoid responsibility. Both approaches have a devastating effect on family relationships because both are prompted by efforts to avoid the responsibilities of family life.

Alcoholics Anonymous is an excellent group to study in

order to understand the character of the alcoholic over and above his drinking. The AA groups are made up of people who, although they are not at the time involved in their drinking practices, are the same kind of people they were when they were drinking. Thus, the AA intergroup structure is much the same as that of the drinking group. One substantial difference lies in the fact that the new sobriety is regarded, deservedly, as being acceptable to others. The AA groups, like the drinking groups, band together for mutual protection and sympathy rather than friendship, and thus give needed support to each other in facing the difficult problem of finding a new life. Often as not, by the time a member has reached the point of seeking AA help, he has estranged himself from other sources of support. Unfortunately, the refuge which AA offers can also give the alcoholic a false sense of security when he yields to the temptation to return to drinking. In a distressingly large number of instances, help is sought only after catastrophic problems have been confronted.

THE INDIVIDUAL ALCOHOLIC

Much of the so-called research being conducted into alcohol involves investigating the effect of alcohol on the body, based on the assumption that alcohol must have a different physiological effect on alcoholics than it has on other people. Such assumptions are in keeping with the excuses offered by the alcoholic for his drinking, but otherwise no evidence is available to support them. Very superficial study of the typical alcoholic reveals that his drinking habits differ from those who use alcohol reasonably only in that one decides to stop drinking after two drinks and the other, consistently, does not stop until

he has had several. In short, the difference is one of judgment. The alcoholic does not seek any different effect from
drinking than other people do and does not experience any
different effect, but only reasons, immaturely, that if two
drinks produce a pleasant feeling, four would yield an
even more desirable one. The problems associated with
excessive drinking are apt to be accumulative, and not so
evident at the beginning. With the passage of time, the
drinking assumes new characteristics. Excesses begin to
earn for the alcoholic the disapproval of others. He frequently interprets this to mean disapproval of his pleasure,
not disapproval of his poor judgment. Because he thinks
that others are out to deny him his pleasure, he is likely
to react rebelliously to this disapproval by carrying his
drinking even further, or at least by drinking in secrecy.

In other words, the study of alcoholism cannot be iso-
lated from studies of the characterological configuration of
the person who becomes alcoholic. When the character
structure of the alcoholic is compared with other people
who have adjustment problems, the similarities are more
apparent than the differences. In other words, it is essentially true, as several reports suggest, that there is no true
"alcoholic personality." Nevertheless, the alcoholic demonstrates very definite and recognizable characteristics that
distinguish him from "normal" people, although not from
all other "abnormal" ones. This fact further substantiates
the contention that the alcoholic person is not a specific
entity, but only a rather accidental by-product of another
problem. The alcoholic can, and often does, take to gambling in the same irrational way that he uses alcohol, and
may alternate one with the other during different periods
of his life, or combine them.

The alcoholic is different from "normal" people in a very
fundamental way, the way in which he characteristically

deals with his responsibilities. His way is immature in that
he consistently fails, on his own, to meet responsibility with
willingness and hard work. When he goes so far as to
avoid responsibility completely and to resort to any device
to justify this avoidance, then he shares the fundamental
characteristic of the schizophrenic, and is, therefore, indistinguishable from the schizophrenic. When this kind of
person comes under the care of a physician, he is known
as a "chronic alcoholic with psychosis." When he does not
go this far, or manages to discharge a minimal amount of
responsibility, then he shares the basic quality of the neurotic, in which case he, too, is a neurotic. Still, he differs
somewhat from most neurotics. He demonstrates, as indicated before, a kind of contempt for the ordinary social
pressures that are effective in making most people conform
to some standard of behavior, whereas the usual neurotic
is likely to enslave himself to these pressures. With this
attitude he demonstrates a kind of rebelliousness toward
society that, at first glance, is somewhat like the sociopath.
The alcoholic, however, expresses his defiance more secretly, and the victim of his irresponsible ways is himself,
and others only indirectly. In other words, he shows a
substantial degree of fear of the very social pressure he
defies. One of the common manifestations of this fear is
his tendency to seek a justification for his unconventional
behavior, and it is his justifications, with all their irrational
logic systems, which form the basis of many of the commonly accepted theories of alcoholism: that the condition
is a "disease," for example, or an "addiction," or that it
is a "defense against unacceptable impulses." The criminal,
on the other hand, does not seek to justify his anti-social
conduct to society at large unless he gets caught, and then
only to avoid punishment. The alcoholic, on the other
hand, is fearful enough of social disapproval to try to jus-

tify his excesses in his own eyes, as well as in the eyes of others. When he completely fails in this effort he gives up trying to remain a part of society and gravitates to a skid row existence. When this occurs, he assumes many of the characteristics of the sociopath in the sense that he makes no further effort to win the approval of others outside his own circle.

In brief, we can say that the typical alcoholic exhibits characteristics that have some similarity to both the neurotic and the sociopath. He is like the former in that he seeks to avoid responsibility and tries to justify his behavior. He is like the latter in that he also defies social pressures. The fact that both sets of characteristics exist in the alcoholic is largely responsible for the fact that he is regarded, by society, as sometimes "sick" and at other times as "bad." There are other types of people who also fall into this middle ground between two extremes of irrational behavior. The homosexual, for example, is a classic example of a blend of the neurotic on the one hand, and, on the other, of the sociopath, in that he confines his antisocial conduct to private practices that only indirectly affect other people. The so-called "drug addict," the type of chronic gambler who impoverishes himself in a senseless and constant effort to recapture his losses, the "respectable" prostitute, the panhandler, the stereotype of the irresponsible "playboy," the person who seeks his livelihood in various and semi-legal kinds of fraud and quackery, the demagogue who trades on people's gullibility for his own ends, are also similar types of character problems, lying midway between "respectable" immaturity and anti-social irresponsibility. Because of the similarities in character structure among these different types, it is not unusual to find individuals shifting from one of these forms of expression to another, or blending two or more of them

in his own person. Also, because they represent this kind
of in-between status as far as respectability is concerned,
different elements in respectable society treat them sometimes as criminals, and at other times as "sick" people.
When the alcoholic "reforms," he may give up the defiant
aspects of his behavior and rely on the more "respectable"
neurotic patterns. Physicians are likely to see him then, as
a hypochondriac, as an ulcer patient, and the like. It is
not unusual for the alcoholic to reform as far as drinking
is concerned and to substitute an excessive preoccupation
with religion. Our modern emphasis on alcoholic rehabilitation programs has provided a new haven for the ex-alco-
holic in which he can engage in public education programs,
fund raising, and other activities in much the same way
that some of the others take to religion. As long as they
manage to get childish gratifications in the form of attention without having to accept very much responsibility,
they may appear to get along rather well. Because their
demands exceed their productiveness, however, their new-
found haven is likely to collapse, thus tempting them to
drink.

One of the well-known traits of the alcoholic, which is
a manifestation of his effort to win approval in spite of
his excessive drinking, is the skill he often develops in
making favorable impressions on others. It is not unusual
to find the alcoholic being a highly entertaining person,
ingratiating and fun-loving. Casual contacts create the impression that he is "likable." But when responsibility and
maturity are demanded of him, he gets into trouble, to his
own, and others', destruction. Like the beautiful woman
whose beauty has made it possible for her to get away
with irrational behavior that other women could not get
away with, the "likableness" of the alcoholic (more evident, of course, early in his life than later) helps him get

away with conduct that others cannot pass off, and this success helps blind him to the long-term pitfalls of his way of living. The trait is especially apt to get him into trouble when he uses it to win positions of high status that then exceed his capacity. When he gets into the highly responsible position, he is likely to carry his drinking beyond his ability to conceal it and thus ruin his career. Biographies of such people are common, and typically fail to equate the changes in drinking with the changes in responsibility.

Chapter

6

PATTERNS OF DRUG USE
AND THE DRUG CULTURE

A COMPREHENSIVE understanding of the current drug abuse problem requires an appreciation of the total cultural setting in which the problem occurs. Those chemical substances that produce comfort or lessen discomfort (e.g. pain) in humans have always been eagerly sought after throughout the history of Western civilization. In medical science, the search for analgesics, sedatives, and anesthetics commanded more attention than any other therapeutic endeavor, and the discoveries made received the most spectacular coverage and recognition. For instance, the following is a list from a book on the history of technology of that author's estimate of the most notable advances made in therapeutic medicine since the beginning of the nineteenth century. Notice the frequency with which those chemicals having comfort-producing properties (indicated by an asterisk) occur in the list.

*Morphine extracted as an active principle from opium in 1805 by a German, Serturner. Became available as a medical remedy after 1821.

Quinine extracted from cinchona bark by Pelletier and Caventon in France in 1818.

*Atropine prepared from belladonna as the active principle by Brandes in 1819.

*Ether first used as an anesthetic in an operation in 1842 by Dr. Long in the United States.

*Chloroform first used as an anesthetic by Sir James Simpson in England.

*Cocaine extracted from Peruvian coca plant by Nieman in 1859 and first used as a local anesthetic in 1884.

Phenol developed by Joseph Lister in England as a surgical antiseptic.

NARCOTIC USE 100 YEARS AGO

"The Brooklyn *Union* in a recent issue gives its readers an account of the extent to which opium is consumed in its city, which may be considered as somewhat astonishing. From $75 to more than $100 per annum is the cost of the opium consumption of single individuals devoted to this habit, from which the quantity they take can be estimated. It is difficult to estimate the aggregate quantity used for purposes of stimulation alone in this country or any section of it. The habit is easier to conceal than the drinking of alcoholic liquors, and statistics are hard to obtain. A country physician once remarked to us that if he could have the exclusive sale of the opium consumed in the single township where he resided, he could make his fortune with charging exaggerated prices."

From Scientific American, *September, 1871.*

*Aspirin synthesized and patented by Herman Dresser, a German in 1893.

Adrenalin extracted from adrenal glands by Takamine and Aldrich in 1901.

*Phenobarbital put on the drug market in 1903.

*Novocaine developed by Alfred Einhorn in 1905 as a local anesthetic.

Salvarsan synthesized by Paul Ehrlich in 1908 as a treatment for syphilis.

Insulin extracted from the pancreas and used in diabetes by Banting and Best in Canada in 1921.

Sulfanilimide (Prontosil) developed by Domagk in Germany in 1935 as an antibiotic.

D.D.T. developed for its insecticide properties in Switzerland by Muller in 1939.

Penicillin discovered by Fleming in England in 1928 but first developed into a practical antibiotic by Howard Flory in 1940.

Streptomycin, another antibiotic, developed by Waksman in 1944 in the United States.

Enovid, introduced in 1960 for its birth control properties, by Gregory Pincus and John Rock in 1957.

MEDICAL SCIENCE AND PUBLIC ATTITUDES

It is interesting to point out that medical science has been primarily interested in finding the causes and cures of diseases. The public, on the other hand, is much more concerned with remedies that will abolish pain, tension, or sleeplessness, and which ultimately have no effect at all on the cure of disease. The marketplace, in other words, demands products quite different from those which

HEROIN ADDICTS FIVE YEARS LATER

Levy attempted to find out what had happened to fifty narcotic addicts who had first contacted a New York City drug clinic five years before (1965). Thirty of the fifty were located and interviewed. Thirty-five were known to be still living in the community, nine were in prison, and six were dead. Nearly all had an arrest record both before and after using drugs. It was concluded that 40 percent were, at the time of follow-up, either non-users of drugs or users of less serious drugs than narcotics. The six deaths represented a 12 percent mortality rate in a five-year period, for a population having an average age of 27.5 years. This is an unusually high rate compared with non-users. Although initially seen in a clinic, the favorable results could not be attributed to this contact.

Author's summary of "Follow-up of 50 Narcotic Addicts," by Barry Levy, in the American Journal of Psychiatry, *January, 1972.*

medical science deems most beneficial in the preservation of life. The role of the marketplace is shown in product advertising. For the past several years, fully one-third of all advertising in medical journals has been to promote the sedatives—analgesics (including the so-called tranquilizers). Before surgical anstisepsis was discovered, surgical anesthetics had been fully developed.

In the public mind, a common theory of medical treatment prevails that fosters a preoccupation with symptomatic remedies and leads to nearly universal acceptance of the prevailing over-medication by physicians. This theory is quite different from those taught and practiced in medical circles. This popular theory might be called the "one-to-one-to-one theory" in that it is based on the assumption that for each symptom that the patient has, there is one corresponding diagnosis appropriate to that symptom, and for each diagnosis there exists a corresponding remedy. This theory is supported by the commonplace finding on the part of people who visit physicians that for every symptom they present, they are given a prescription.

In view of the vast outpouring of therapeutic agents during the present century, it might appear that there is a remedy for every symptom that people experience. The truth, in fact, is that only a relatively small number of effective remedies exist that have a direct influence in altering the course of an illness. Belief in the efficacy of these many other remedies, however, is sustained by the fact that most of the time, people who describe symptoms to a physician do, indeed, get over them. Almost invariably the credit is given to the last remedy tried. Actually, many of the symptoms that people present are not indicative of disease and many others indicate self-limiting conditions that run their course regardless of what measures are taken to remedy them. In both cases, the symptoms disappear regardless of remedies, although it seems to be invariably the case that the remedy gets the credit. Of the remaining cases, there are two groups, one for which effective remedies are available and capable of producing sometimes dramatic relief of symptoms (but through a cure of the disease, not mere abolition of symptoms); and the other comprising those conditions for which there is no remedy, and which continue to progress, perhaps eventually proving fatal. In any unselected⁴ sample of patients seeking medical attention, probably not more than 5 or 10 percent belong to that fortunate group that has a condition that is curable by an available remedy. The first two groups, those having no disease and those having self-limiting conditions, would make up, altogether, about 80 percent of the total, leaving the remainder in that group of seriously ill for whom no treatment measures exist. The kind of reasoning employed by the public, however, is based on a different view of these statistics than an objective medical view would consist of. The typical patient population sees, instead, that some 85 to 90 percent of people with symptoms seeking help end up, after taking some remedy, free of the symptoms. It seems clear to them that the remedy was the responsible agent. In the old days when fewer remedies were available, many people with symptoms did not seek help, so this group served as a control of untreated cases. Today, however, the general impression gained by an observer of America's health practices indi-

FREQUENCY OF DRUG USE IN A HIGH SCHOOL POPULATION

318 high school students surveyed in Florida in 1971. 24% of the total had used illegal drugs once or more.

DRUG USED	NEVER USED	USED ONCE	USED MORE
Marijuana	8%	28%	64%
Hallucinogens	64	16	19
Amphetamines	55	23	22
Barbiturates	60	18	22
Opiates	88	9	3
Glue	65	29	6

From Patterns of Drug Use in a High School Population, *Jose Lombillo, M.D. and Jack Hain, Ph.D.,* American Journal of Psychiatry, *January, 1972.*

cates that no such control group exists anymore—that is, there appears to be no significant group of people who have symptoms but do not get some remedy—all of which robs others of the opportunity of having a control group for comparison.

The health consciousness of the American population is deep-seated, pervasive, and often assumes the proportions of a religious dedication. It is identified in the public mind with highly respected sciences and technology, and is especially brought to bear on the issue of raising children. Young mothers tend to become unusually interested in, and often quite sophisticated about, matters of health. A measure of this trend is shown by the increase from 60 percent to 99 percent of the children born in hospitals during the last forty years. In some ways, however, it might be said that in this context, "a little knowledge is a dangerous thing," because it is derived from the naïve kind of

ON TRANQUILIZERS

".... It's clear already that a lot of people are gunning for the new [tranquilizer] drugs. According to a prominent New York Medical authority, promiscuous use of such drugs may be a 'dangerous threat to national health, more than cancer ever will be.' "

Business Week, September, 1956.

".... The Committee's attention was drawn to the very rapidly increasing use of those agents which are being described as 'tranquilizers' and 'ataraxics.' The Committee believed that these substances, diverse in their chemical characteristics, but similar in their central sedative action, must be classed as potentially habit forming. In addition, some evidence has been presented that, under conditions of excessive use, a characteristic with-drawal syndrome can appear. . . . In this respect, the 'tranquilizers' and 'ataraxics' resemble the barbituates and should be subjected to national control."

Seventh Report of the Expert Committee on Addic-tion-Producing Drugs of the World Health Organiza-tion, 1957.

". . . . Very soon, the drugs were prescribed in private practice for the many who were seeking relief from anxiety and tension. Their usage in this area has been on a gigantic scale. The American Psychiatric Association has stated that 35 million prescriptions for these drugs will be written in 1956, and that of 10 compounds most frequently prescribed by physicians in 1955, 3 were tran-quilizers (and this was the first year they were introduced). . . . An additional aspect of the situa-tion is the extravagant and distorted literature which some of the drug houses are distributing to the medical profession."

Committee on Public Health, New York Academy of Medicine, 1956.

". . . . While some of the initial blatant excesses have undoubtedly subsided, the subcommittee heard sufficient testimony based on tranquilizing drug advertising in current professional journals and direct mail advertising material to indicate that deceptive advertising of these drugs is still a serious problem."

From the subcommittee's report.

"There exists in the lay minds the belief that the tranquilizers are a cure-all for any and every emo-tional disorder. This trend is enhanced by the physician who prescribes a few of the pills with the attitude that they will do no harm even if they do no good. This is an attitude that should be condemned. There is no short-cut to psychotherapy. Since the advent of the tranquilizers, the overall tendency has been to use them as substitutes for the time-consuming business of investigation of the patient's reaction to his environment."

Editorial from the Arkansas Medical Society Journal, *March, 1963.*

"One out of six Americans today uses the pill bottle to change his mental attitudes and perceptions. This almost slavish dependence on medication by 30 million Americans has become one of the most serious and pressing problems of our time. Doctors and health authorities are appalled by the constantly broadening scope of the new drug kick. Teenagers and college students are indulging in wild orgiastic binges with the most powerful compounds ever known to mankind."

Robert Goldman, The Ladies Home Journal, *October, 1963.*
Excerpts from testimony submitted to the U.S. Senate "Kefauver" drug hearings, U.S. Government Printing Office, 1963.

theorizing we have just mentioned. As a result, the vast majority of the population is over-medicated and the notion that for every problem there is a pharmacological remedy is perpetuated. No generation of Americans has been so imbued with this philosophy, and with the drug-taking practices surrounding it than those who have been parents following the post World War II years. Today's growing drug abuse problem tends to involve primarily the children of these parents, and the similarities in drug orientation are much more striking than the differences.

A subsidiary phenomenon has come to be associated

with this growing faith and dependency on pharmocology. Aided and abetted by movies, television, and advertising barrages, but finding a willing acceptance in the minds and hearts of millions of people, there has developed a new attitude in the country toward experiencing any kind of discomfort. No longer is discomfort merely discomfort; it is now a calamity. People now demand such exquisite control, for instance, of environmental temperature that any deviation of a few degrees from the optimum 70° is regarded as catastrophic. Any degree of pain is looked upon as something requiring immediate, emergency attention. Tension and anxiety are discomforts to be avoided at all costs. No longer is the endurance of hardship a sign of manhood, or "good for building character," or a sign of heroism. Relief or avoidance of any of these types of discomforts is widely assumed to depend on some appropriate drug, and this attitude—ensuring against suffering— prompts a great deal of the drug use now going on. A measure of this attitude is the prevalence of supplies of various such drugs in peoples' homes.

It is no wonder, then, that our adolescents, when confronted with the inevitable anxieties of growing up, look for, and think they find, relief through drugs—sometimes prescribed by accommodating physicians, sometimes obtained through extra-legal channels. Furthermore, it is also no wonder that these same young people look upon themselves as infinitely more sophisticated about the whole drug issue than the "squares" who are preaching against it, meanwhile consuming huge quantities of their particular brands of tension-relieving, or comfort-promoting, chemicals. They claim to see and understand better than older people their elders' blind hypocrisy about the issue —and use this alleged insight to justify their doing the same foolish things.

MARIHUANA AND HEALTH: A REPORT TO THE CONGRESS

"It is important that we learn more about the possible interactions between the use of marihuana and a wide range of other drugs. This includes not only such drug substances as caffein, tobacco, and alcohol, but also other drugs that are abused and a wide spectrum of drugs employed therapeutically. As marihuana comes to be used by a wider spectrum of the population, it is important that we learn its effects on those whose physiological functioning is impaired to some degree or who suffer from physical or psychological disabilities. Such effects must be studied over a wide dosage range and in various use patterns.

"From a psychosocial point of view it is essential that we come to better understand the different patterns of drug use, their implications for social functioning, and the factors that contribute to such use. These include parental attitudes, child-rearing practices, and peer pressures as well as those aspects of subcultural and cultural practices that may affect use. Finally, it is imperative that we determine prevention and education techniques that will be more effective in averting drug abuse of all types, including that of marihuana."

From a report by the Secretary of Health, Education and Welfare, January, 1971.

DRUG MYTHOLOGIES

Many of the current social problems that now trouble the nation, such as crime and violence, are very ancient, in spite of the impression given in the news media that they have only recently materialized. Because they are ancient, such issues are surrounded by mystery, folklore, and myths that impede rational attempts to understand and solve them. Over-simplification and over-generalization tend to be principal ways of distorting complex issues. For example, the war on poverty sees poverty, simplistically, as merely an economic issue, one that can be solved by raising incomes.

The issue at hand—social problems involving drug use —is a striking case in point. Our problem in setting up effective programs is being seriously impeded by the mythologies that prevail about the subject. The prevailing myths not infrequently obtain such widespread support that they lead to the establishment of elaborate legal machinery and laws—which, no matter how ineffective they prove to be, continue in force.

For instance: As one studies the history of the American people during the present century, it would be easy to reach the conclusion that, at least, the people learned one important lesson following a certain experiment. They clearly learned, one would suppose, the utter futility of making liquor prohibition work—and the ultimate repeal of the Eighteenth Amendment after experimenting with prohibition for fourteen years would indicate that we truly learned this lesson. Nevertheless, immediately after repeal we set up the same system in an attempt to control drug use and have ever since been encountering the same kinds of failures. Drug prohibition has been organized and enforced in precisely the same way that liquor prohibition was, and with the same dismal results, in spite of the obvious fact that the problems are nearly identical. As a result of our failure, we have created an enforcement system that encourages rather than discourages drug use— one that brings huge profits to illegal merchants working

WOMEN AND DRUGS:
WARNING IN A RECENT POPULAR
MAGAZINE

"Are you chronically tired?
Do you feel increasingly unattractive?
Are the children driving you wild?
Do routine chores seem insuperable?
Are you anxious, irritable, depressed?
Do you want to crawl into a hole?

"If you answer yes to any of the above questions,
watch out. You may end up hooked on legal mood-
altering drugs, popping tranquilizers and other
potentially dangerous pills that might cause serious
illness and sometimes death. And they will all be
legal—prescribed by your own family doctor."

From Roland Berg, "The Over-Medicated Woman,"
McCall's, September, 1971.

within the framework of organized crime, one that breeds
corruption of police and politicians, and one that, above
all, intensifies the disrespect of law and order that began
during the early prohibition days. The essence of mythology or religion lies in the readiness of people to believe
in them in spite of evidence to the contrary. In connection
with our present system of drug prohibition, there exists
a widespread faith in the system—in spite of a general
awareness that the system is not working, and in spite of
the fact that the same people who support the system will
readily admit that national attempts at liquor prohibition
were failures. There is no apparent awareness abroad in
the country, however, of the evident contradictions.

The myths and distortions abroad concerning drug abuse

THE MARIHUANA MYSTIQUE AND CULTURE

The uniqueness of marihuana use is manifested by the following aspects of a prevailing set of practices:

1. The drug is typically used in a group.
2. The other persons in the group are either socially intimate, or potential members of the social group, not strangers.
3. The relations among members are long-term continuing social relations.
4. The group shares many common values.
5. As the group evolves, values tend to converge toward greater congruance.
6. The group constantly re-affirms its solidarity.
7. The activity of drug smoking becomes the unifying mark of identification, by which the members define themselves.

Author's summary of E. Goode, The Marijuana Market, The Columbia Forum, *Winter, 1969.*

---

are not the sole province of the ignorant and the uneducated. Quite the contrary. Many that currently influence social policy originated within the medical profession itself. As a matter of fact, there is a growing and nagging suspicion that an important root of our current drug problem —at least a partial cause of the whole mess—came from standard and accepted medical practice. Some of the concepts prevailing in medicine that have been influential are as follows:

1. Starting in the mid-1950s, the drug manufacturers hit upon a profit bonanza that rapidly became their major

source of income. They flooded the market with a vast
array of new drugs to which they affixed the term "tranquilizers." Although there was nothing either new or remarkable about the pharmacological effects of these drugs
—since they generally had the same effects as the well-
established barbituates—the drug companies launched a
massive advertising campaign designed to promote the idea
that a pharmacological Utopia had arrived. To a considerable extent, this campaign succeeded, and a new drug
mythology has become firmly embedded in the American
folklore, aided and abetted by physicians and nurses and
conveniently spread to the masses by movies and television.
This folklore states that for any given state of anguish,
sorrow, disappointment, frustration, or resentment, there
exists a way of attaining euphoric release through drugs.

These so-called tranquilizers were first introduced in
1955 by only a couple of drug companies (a conspicuous
leader being the one that for years had been promoting
Carters' Little Liver Pills). Only one year later, in 1956,
the total sales of these drugs had reached $125 million
annually and by 1962 the figure had doubled. As early as
1959, a survey of a group of Wall Street executives disclosed that one-third had been given prescriptions for these
drugs by their physicians. The percentage of the population that has, by now, been given these drugs is not known,
but probably comes close to 90 percent.

2. As the use of these drugs spread, their obvious dangers and disastrous side effects became increasingly apparent, although never in a way that led to any reduction in
their use. For instance, as early as 1957, the WHO Committee on Addiction-Producing Drugs recommended that
these drugs be included in the dangerous list. In 1962, the
U.N. Commission on Narcotics added them to the list.
Meanwhile, a growing list of automobile accidents, sui-
cides, industrial accidents, and at least two airplane acci-

dents were seen to be related to use of these agents. Never, however, have these warnings had any effect on the flagrant claims being made by the advertisers or on the reckless abandon with which they have been prescribed by M.D.'s. It is surely more than a coincidence that the growing number of young people now taking illegal drugs are the sons and daughters of parents who have been taught during the past fifteen years to solve their emotional problems with tranquilizers—by respected physicians and nurses. These events are cited to illustrate what the current drug mythology means—namely, a resilient faith in the efficacy of these drugs in the face of a growing body of evidence that they yield grossly contradictory effects.

3. Another myth endorsed by the medical profession and widely accepted by the public states that of many chemical agents having essentially the same effect on the people who ingest them, some are "safe" and others are not, some are "addicting" and others are not, some have valuable medical qualities and others do not. These chemicals include: (a) the tranquilizers, (b) the barbituates and other old-fashioned sedatives, (c) marihuana, (d) morphine and heroin, and (e) alcohol. In fact, there is little to distinguish any members on this list from the others, and the fact that one might be taken after being prescribed by a physician while another is purchased on the black market does not magically change its effects. In the same way, the fact that middle-aged bankers consume one kind at a fashionable cocktail party and young people use a bootleg product at a less fashionable party does not magically make one safe and the other unsafe. Actually, the only rational objection that can be leveled at the bootlegging of marihuana (if we accept the fashionable cocktail party as a standard of legitimacy) is that the product is probably over-priced and of inferior quality.

4. Many other myths are promulgated by the medical

profession and accepted on faith by the public, not the least of which is the concept of addiction itself. This point will be elaborated on elsewhere in this report; suffice it to say, meanwhile, that the standard concept of addiction as promoted by physicians is one taken over unmodified from the so-called addicts themselves. In other words, physicians have accepted at face value the theories presented to them by addicts, and the public, in turn, has taken them at face value from physicians.

THE OLD NARCOTIC SUB-CULTURE

Apparently coincident with the appearance and flourishing of our modern-type, big-city slum since the 1930s, largely stimulated by migration of southern poor whites and blacks to the large cities, where welfare benefits were superior to those in the rural south, a narcotic-using sub-culture developed. These slums previously housed the lower-class working people and newly arrived immigrants from Europe, but as both groups became somewhat more affluent and mobile, they moved to better housing at the fringes of the cities, while the middle class that previously inhabited those areas moved to the suburbs. World War II saw a major expansion in these ghetto communities, both in the number of cities containing them and in the size of each one, because of the expansion of job opportunities. Many forces work to create, perpetuate, and expand ghetto communities, and the simplistic view that poverty alone is a determining factor is short-sighted. In a sense, it might be said that there exists a "critical mass effect" in these areas, in that once they acquire a certain optimum size or density of population there is thereby generated a momentum that not only sustains them but also determines the direction of development. For instance, when a certain set of boundaries become established around a ghetto, a wall of resistance seems to be built up around it to contain it within these boundaries. This wall acts like a dam that permits pressures to build up until finally it bursts out explosively and spills over large areas of additional territory. The screening process by which populations are admitted or rejected in the ghetto community serve to make for a homogeneity of people not seen elsewhere, where screening processes are not so rigid. An architectural study was once conducted to establish what factors determined whether or not a given fringe area in a large city became a part of the ghetto. The conclusion was that an irreversible change occurred in a given block adjacent to the ghetto when landlords began collecting rents on a weekly instead of monthly basis. This finding is consistent with the common observation that ghetto residents, either by design or force of economic circumstances, are usually ready to move within a few days' notice, as well as that they typically refrain from making plans, commitments, or amassing the capital needed to plan as far ahead as one month. There always exists in the ghetto an anonymity that attracts people looking for anonymity. Finding a place where one's identity can be concealed is possible only when a certain "critical mass" is achieved. At that point, the inhabitants of the ghetto all begin to look alike to outsiders, including the police. In any event, a prevailing phenomenon of ghetto life is the alienation, the disenfranchisement that comes with this anonymity.

It appears to have been among this group of people particularly that narcotic use became a way of life and led to the establishment of the old narcotic sub-culture. The membership came to be selected from among the least ambitious, most passive, most dependent persons who had

a deep disinterest in working for a living, few if any plans
for the future, and nothing but immediate pleasure as a
motive for living. The traffickers in narcotics were available in the ghetto, and relied on these people as their
customers. Certain basic skills were needed in the area of
petty theft to get the means of buying drugs, but, otherwise, they tended to live on a day-to-day basis, largely
forgotten and ignored by everybody else. The size and
impact of this group has probably remained rather constant,
and the recent upsurge in the magnitude and character of
the drug problem includes this group only by accident.
This group, for instance, was probably responsible for very
little spread of narcotic use, for their drug use tended to
be solitary and placed no premiums on others participating.

It is this old narcotic sub-culture that is referred to in
the Bureau of Narcotics reports, the Bureau itself having
disappeared from the scene recently with the new turn of
events in drug use. In a sense, the Bureau and this group
of narcotic users, mostly confined to a few large city ghet-
tos, achieved a kind of symbiotic relationship, or equilibrium, each sustaining the other while also serving to
impose some degree of restriction on expansion. In other
words, they seem almost to have existed for each other.
Now, enforcement is in the Department of Justice, and the
old philosophy of the Bureau (part of the Treasury Department) has begun to wane as new styles of drug use and
abuse sweep the country.

OTHER NARCOTIC GROUPS

The old sub-culture does not account for all
the users of hard narcotics, but an uncertain, smaller number exist in a scattered fashion diffused throughout the

population. Their lack of high density in any area prevents them from assuming the characteristics of a sub-culture. One of these groups has always been around, and has probably been declining rather than increasing in numbers. These are the people who have become addicted to morphine as a result of medical treatment, in which case their original introduction to the use of narcotics, and probably their continued use of them, has been brought about by physicians. As a result, this is the group physicians are likely to be most familiar with. Physicians are generally taught to be alert to the possibilities of introducing patients to narcotics addiction, for the ones likely to follow this route are fairly easily identified. They are typically people (more often women than men) who have passive, dependent personalities, who tend to become easily alarmed over minor discomforts, who have already in the past shown a tendency to over-use medications (or alcohol), and who tend to exhibit unusual (immature) reactions to the effects of drugs. Nevertheless, the administration of a sedative or analgesic drug to a patient who is anxiously demanding it too often appears to the physician as the easiest way to get the problem off his hands. These people typically use an assortment of physical complaints with suitable heart-rending embellishments to justify a physician's continuing to administer the drugs; so after appropriate shopping around, these people usually manage to find some physician who will accommodate them. These physicians, then, tend to acquire a local reputation as being free in prescribing these drugs and thus tend to attract more customers. The allegation that these physicians follow this route for profit is probably a mistake. More often, it appears that the physician is one who is susceptible to the kind of blackmail these people learn to employ. This group has the advantage of not participating in the blackmarket in narcotics.

Another group of narcotics users appears, now, to be

spreading in a rather random distribution among the larger drug cultures. Given a certain rather large number of youthful drug users, most of whom use marihuana, a certain small number will end up using narcotics. How this happens, why it happens, and how they get involved in the blackmarket traffic is unclear at this time, for the principal outlets for the heroin retail trade do not seem to be extensive enough to permit it to happen.

THE MARIHUANA SUB-CULTURE(S)

Marihuana use can no longer be said to be confined to a single sub-culture but, rather, there appears to have developed more than one type. The original marihuana culture was more restricted and clearly defined. It appears to have developed during the 1930s within a certain limited world of popular musicians at a time when popular music was taking the new turn into improvisation and emphasis on the individual soloist. These musicians typically led a nomadic life, confining their associations to people who had styles of work and living entirely different from the rest of society, often coming in contact with the underworld as a result of playing in speakeasies, and largely unhampered by any guides to conduct that most other people followed. Pleasure seeking, adventure, and a general disregard for convention became dominant. It became easy for them to convince one another that they had special insights into life and self-expression, and that these were enhanced under the influence of marihuana. As such, the drug use served an occupational objective by making them better musicians, at least in their own eyes. After a period of apparent quiescence around the time of World War II, marihuana use was re-invented by new groups of

people in the fifties and sixties who, in the process, re-dis-
covered the wonderful effects that marihuana was supposed
to have had in the past.

It will be useful to draw some comparisons with alcohol drinking patterns. In the case of drinking, it can be
safely concluded that there exists in the American culture
at least three rather distinct groups of users. First is that
large group of the majority of the population that uses alcohol reasonably. That is to say, these people use alcohol
from time to time, but in no way does this use constitute
a problem as defined by society. Second, at the other extreme, is the group of some 10 million or so alcoholics
whose use of alcohol is clearly irrational, and, as a result,
constitutes serious problems. A third group, not commonly
recognized, is made up of people who use alcohol, not to
the extent to which the alcoholic does, but in a way that
more or less accidently leads to problems. The typical example of this group would be the young teenager who
never becomes an alcoholic, but whose inexperience and
struggles to demonstrate his masculinity put him behind
the steering wheel of an automobile while intoxicated, thus
producing the ingredients of tragic accidents. Both automobiles and alcohol share the same properties. They have
such a degree of power for destruction that in the hands
of the inexperienced they always constitute a potential
hazard. Furthermore, the combination of the two can be
particularly lethal.

The general public conception of marihuana users has
been that they all belong to the same kind of a category
that would be equivalent to alcoholics. That is to say, the
concept of there being a similar set of three categories
among marihuana users ranging from a reasonable to an
irrational extreme has not been generally considered. This
tendency to generalize, and to treat all marihuana users

alike, contributes to much of the current misunderstanding. It apparently seems so inconceivable to many people that there might exist a class of rational users of the drug that the question is not even entertained, in spite of the fact that reasonable versus irrational use of alcohol is widely understood. To a large extent, this over-generalization stems from the ease and readiness with which the American public, especially as it is represented by the press, identifies phenomena with simplistic labels. For instance, of all the many characteristics and qualities that might be used to describe a certain class of young people, the fact that some of them might use marihuana becomes sufficient for labeling the entire group this way. With the label, then, there is conjured up a whole list of assumptions and prejudices, all based on the fact that it is a different and strange class of people that is being considered, and that drug use is the cause, not an effect.

In spite of this public tendency, it is now quite evident that marihuana users comprise more than one sub-group, and that the same three classes into which alcohol users can be grouped can be used to classify marihuana users. For example, recent trends indicate that there are many, perhaps the vast majority of, marihuana users whose use of the drug does not appear to differ significantly from the way in which many people smoke tobacco.

The spread of marihuana use in the U.S. during the past fifteen years has been a result of an extension of the practice into new and different communities (no longer found almost exclusively in large metropolitan centers), new age groups of both sexes (tending toward younger groups), and into upper socio-economic groups. At least one effect of this spread has been to make the marihuana sub-culture much less homogenous in its characteristics than it was before. Until very recently, at least one common bond held marihuana users together and served to screen in certain members while screening out others. This bond was the illegal nature of using or being in the possession of the drug. In some communities, however, a kind of tacit pact has been arrived at with local authorities who agree to leave the users to their own devices in return for their confining their activities to certain restricted portions of the community. This kind of arrangement is essentially the one made in many communities with prostitutes, and was the prevailing approach used toward liquor during prohibition days. In these cases, then, marihuana users in certain areas can feel quite immune to prosecution or police attention, and thus the common bond of law defiance becomes correspondingly diminished. On the college campus, on the other hand, the police appear to be more willing to make this kind of arrangement. In some cases, it appears that part of the game consists of defying the law, so that a certain amount of police attention is welcomed. As the marihuana movement (for this is almost what it has become) has progressed, the illegality appears to be both less important as a reason for use, and less important as a reason for avoiding use. A recent survey of a group of youths that was prejudged to be the most establishment-oriented, most conventional, most law-abiding that could be identified—namely, the law students in the University of California—revealed that 73 percent of them had tried marihuana at one time. This seems indicative of a prevailing attitude on the part of youth to de-emphasize the illegality of use, in spite of the fact that there has appeared to be no abatement of public sentiment for prohibition.

A feature of the marihuana traffic that sharply distinguishes it from heroin traffic is one which casts the issue in a light much different from what the public believes. The public, in general, and legislators, in particular, seem to see

little or no difference between heroin and marihuana use
(or abuse). One of the alarms expressed over the use of
drugs is the exposure that the users get to the underworld
that allegedly handles the traffic. The facts are, however,
that heroin distribution does clearly appear to be largely
a monopoly of syndicated crime organizations, but the vast
majority of marihuana traffic (except perhaps importation)
is still in the hands of amateurs. This fact is an indication
of how relatively easy it is to distribute and sell the drug.

Perhaps the best-known marihuana sub-culture is the
prevalent one that uses the drug for party or socializing
purposes. Typically, the people in this group are quite
young, interested in experimenting, looking for excitement,
and in a mood to celebrate. The acquisition by one member
of a supply becomes the usual excuse for holding a "pot"
party. The behavior of the members at these parties is
dictated by a rigid protocol that dictates members' responses
and behavior. The novice, without this pre-training, is unaware of how smoking the drug leaf will affect him and requires proper guidance before he responds in the accepted
way. As might be expected, inexperienced users will get the
same effect from placebos, if the proper social setting is
provided. Chances are that a very large majority of this
group of users experiment very irregularly or for only a
very few times, and could not be considered regular users.
Each party, for instance, is likely to be the occasion for
introducing new members. The romantically structured
ceremony of the pot party has produced a variety of poetic
descriptions of the experience, the vividness of the imagery
probably being more a product of the poetic talents of the
writers than a product of the drug effects. The poetry,
however, tends to institutionalize the tradition.

It is not unusual for the alleged effects of an intoxicant
to be a result of the setting in which it is used rather than

to the actual pharmacological effects of the chemical. Typically, for instance, different kinds of drinking parties produce different kinds of reactions—a polite and aristocratic cocktail party differing, thus, from a victory celebration after a football game.

In any event, the group of young people who participate in the party-type of marihuana use appear to be no different in character from a group that might, instead, attend a beer party. The description thus presented might appear to place this use of marihuana in an innocuous light, but this is not intended. The fact that much of what does happen under these circumstances is quite harmless does not mean there are no hazards connected with it. Some of the participants are clearly too immature, too irresponsible, to manage the kind of responsibility needed to deal with drug use rationally, and these would clearly be the ones tempted to go along with the others, and then go along to more serious kinds of behavior. However, if marihuana parties were not available to them, they would undoubtedly have found a similar route to destructive ends—through beer, for example.

Another sub-group of marihuana users are the regulars who might smoke the drug almost daily for several years. This group is probably a more homogenous one, with more distinguishing characteristics. These are the people for whom the drug is a ticket of admission into a culture that they seek for reasons other than use of the drug or any benefits they get from the drug. The drug is the ticket because it symbolizes an anti-establishment set of values that is carefully designed to contrast with what is adolescently conceived of as middle-class-Protestant-Anglo-Saxon-puritanism. For the most part, the culture is a negative image of the alleged establishment in that it is filled with many prohibitions against doing the things supposedly characteristic of the establishment, with a minimum of newly created substitutes to take their place. By default more than by design, the standard of conduct then becomes "doing one's thing"—spontaneous, creative, individualized self-expression—all of which can easily capture the fancies of those who think they have been disillusioned by traditional values. Study of some of these individuals reveal often that their real disillusionment is not directed against the Great Society, for they really know very little about it, but against their own parents. Too often, their parents have been people who have either exercised neglect or a tyrannical control over their children, but meanwhile have used establishment-type moralisms to enforce their control. The children then blame the resultant lack of cooperation and comradeship, not on the tyranny or the preaching, but on the establishment that the parents claim to represent.

The daring quality of marihuana experimentation, with the sense of thrill and excitement associated with novelty and adventure is, apparently, coming to be more and more a characteristic of rather young users, at the high school level, whereas the somewhat older users who have had the experience tend to treat the experience much less dramatically. Still, there seems to exist a cultism, a mystique, which those who use the drug become immersed in. They tend to picture themselves as members of a kind of closed fraternity who possess superior insights and intellectual powers, and outsiders, especially the police, are looked upon as "stupid," naive, "square." The police are familiar with these attitudes and are likely to find themselves uncomfortable in the face of them; and thus tend to set themselves up as rivals to the cult. Other offenders that the police have dealings with look upon the police with honest hostility or fear, but not with superior contempt. The efforts the youthful marihuana users exert to outwit the police are countered by efforts on the police's part in turn to outwit them. In some communities, these counter-acting forces begin to look equally adolescent.

The so-called "hippie" style of life has become a sub-sub-culture that tends to carry to extremes the traditions being established in the cult. In some cases, constructive growth has occurred as some of these groups break off to form more or less workable communes that are self-supporting and that make a systematic effort to construct a genuine life of simplicity. More often, however, membership in the hippie communities is temporary during adolescence, or is an attempt to escape from the hopelessness of a ghetto existence, or is regarded as a haven by young people who are determined to spend the rest of their lives without any accouterments of responsibility.

In a sense, the mystique that these young people have generated for themselves has become a kind of bluff that they are being called upon more and more to carry out. They rationalize their choices on the grounds of freeing themselves from the slavery of middle-class standards in order to be creative and independent. Having justified their choices on these grounds, and not having encountered the massive attacks they expected against this philosophy, many of them are actually seeking ways of finding simpler lives through creative independence. Adolescents have long been noted for their tendency to seek unconventional modes of expression, only to find themselves conforming much more rigidly to the conventions they devise than the ones they are forsaking. Their efforts to be independent typically take the half-way step of avoiding doing what others expect, but without creating something better to take its place. As a result, their creativity looks remarkably stereotyped, following fleeting fashions in a slavish way and producing merely a shift in their dependencies. Those adolescents

whose growing-up struggles take these forms are characteristically the ones inhabiting the sub-culture in question.

Some interesting studies have been reported on groups
of drug users who have participated in treatment-rehabilita-
tion programs (Synanon, Daytop Village, Teen Challenge,
Washington Heights Rehabilitation Center). When studied
in groups, it has been observed that the young people who
abandon the use of hard drugs, but who maintain group
associations afterward in the treatment programs, very
much resemble Alcoholics Anonymous groups. In both
cases, the culture they structure and maintain is essentially
unchanged, whether they are on drugs or not, indicating
that the phenomenon of drug (or alcohol) use or abuse was
incidental, and only important in having brought them
together. A dominant theme is the yearning for a life of
diminished responsibility, and the life styles and phi-
losophies that develop tend to be rationalizations for the
avoidance of responsibility.

THE "TRANQUILIZED" SUB-CULTURE

In 1955, the class of drugs now known as
"tranquilizers" was placed on the ethical drug market
(ethical meaning that distribution and advertising is restricted to physician prescription channels). The choice of
name for this group of drugs was cleverly contrived, and
violated a tradition in the ethical drug field that forbids the
sale of drugs under names that convey implications about
their effects. Other names competed for attention—such as
"psychotropic drugs"—but the first name captured the
public fancy so solidly that this is the one that survived the
competition. The rapid market success of these drugs is
attributable mostly to the skillful advertising used, which

was designed to leak out of medical and into lay channels in order to create a public demand as well as a medical demand.

Although never advertised or sold as such, and not even regarded in most medical circles as such, they have been found to have essentially the same effects on humans as the barbituate drugs, which have been available since the beginning of this century. In other words, they act as depressants to the brain. Advertising claims falsely insist that they do not make people drowsy. The truth is that the sleep-inducing (hypnotic) effect is merely a dosage phenomenon, being not very evident in small doses, but increasing with larger ones. In spite of the fact that the pharmacologic effect is indistinguishable from other, older sedatives, clever advertising has created the legend that they possess other, apparently magical, properties.

It is interesting that most medical journals manage to survive financially because of the heavy advertising income they receive from the many manufacturers of these drugs. It is commonly believed by those whose sympathies do not lie solidly with the drug companies or their products that this generous advertising revenue has purchased a great deal of medical good-will for the drugs, far out of proportion to their medical value. As a result, some claim that the worthy medical journals very seldom, if ever, publish any information that discredits the class of drugs as a whole, although an increasingly long list of individual ones has come to be associated with undesirable side effects. Several have already been taken off the market, but the number available has not dropped appreciably. The abuse potential and the undesirable side effects are seldom apparent when these drugs are first introduced on the market, but seem, inevitably, to accrue with time. The World Health Organization, as a result, has placed them on the list of "dangerous drugs," and the new 1971 federal laws place new and additional controls over them.

The clever advertising already mentioned has been meant to, and has succeeded in, creating the impression in the minds of an already receptive medical and lay public that these drugs will relieve anxiety and the other unpleasant emotional reactions people are prone to have. No significant amount of influence has yet been brought to bear to the effect: (1) that this might not be true, or (2) if true, it might not be a desirable thing to do to people. Instead, both of these propositions have been widely accepted in the positive, and any debate that arises involves the pros and cons of a particular choice of one of these drugs over another.

Drug companies are known to spend on advertising an average of $3,000 per year per every physician in the United States, one-third of which is directed to tranquilizer–sedative–analgesic drugs. Advertising budgets of drug companies represent about 10 percent of gross sales, and their highly promoted "research" gets 5 percent. Probably, however, the greatest salesmen for these drugs have been professional entertainers who, since 1955, have contributed heavily to the favorable folklore concerning them. Entertainers themselves tend to be heavy users of the drugs. This indirect but highly effective way of reaching the consumer assures that if a physician does not recommend one of these drugs to a patient, there is a good chance that the patient will propose it himself.

The same placebo effect that epitomizes the marihuana mystique typifies the tranquilizers. Because large segments of the population have already been led to form favorable opinions through the mass media, and because physicians tend to reinforce the optimism of the patient with his own confidence, the patient often does, indeed, seem to experience the desired effect—to relax. The uncomfortable sensations that the drugs are alleged to relieve are usually sufficiently fleeting and vague that almost any effect can easily be interpreted as the desired one. This set of conditions, however, is the perfect culture medium to nurture the problem of drug abuse. And so the tranquilizers have become, in numbers of people affected, second only to alcohol in creating new victims, far more than the number of young people using marihuana. There are two glaring and overpowering factors responsible for the continued use and abuse of these drugs: (1) the public wants the kinds of effects they promise, and (2) physicians want the kind of remedy to prescribe that these drugs propose to be. These factors are sufficiently powerful to make it virtually impossible to bring about any measurable counter-influence. Not mentioned, but also of some consequence, is the fact that these drugs have been more profitable to the manufacturers than anything else they turn out (more so than the vitamins, which touched off an earlier craze, and the antibiotics). Their profitability lies in the fact that people have accepted the necessity of paying rather high prices for them (blackmarket prices once reached $1 per capsule), whereas, in the case of vitamins, they demanded bargains.

More aften than not the user and the abuser of tranquilizers is a woman rather than a man, mostly because more women than men visit physicians (by a wide margin). She may be of any age. She is likely to be in contact with other women in her circle who also take, or have taken, these drugs, for it would be almost impossible to find in any group of more than three women today one who has not tried them. The use of the drugs is not confined to those obtained by doctor's prescriptions, for many homes are equipped with a surplus to give to friends, and women often come to regard themselves as having some degree of expertise in prescribing. One gets the impression from studying some of these drug-sharing practices that many of the women justify using them on themselves to the degree to which they help others find access to them. Typically, the woman user attributes her reason for taking them not to the internal sense of discomfort from tension, but to the presence of what she regards as external stress. Stress to vast numbers of women consists of nothing more commonplace than crying babies or household boredom. The alcoholic is also likely to use similar tactics—that is, to justify his own excesses by enticing others into sharing his drinking.

Men and career women are not immune to the uses and abuses of these drugs, but seem more likely to appreciate the fact that a cocktail can be more fun and have the same effect. Men do not seem to be as ready as women to share their drug use, not so likely to compare notes with one another, and more likely to keep their drug use a secret.

A drug-taking ritual has become well established in extensive portions of the population whereby almost any of the commonplace crises of life are automatically regarded as something to be overcome by taking tranquilizers. In other populations, or in the same population at other times, the same occasions would call for a therapeutic drink of alcohol. A prevailing attitude that is used to rationalize these practices is a strange distortion of the American tradition of respect for hard work. Almost invariably, it seems, the current rationalizations for drug use begin with some sort of claim that the person has endured the stresses and pressures of work, of responsibility, of self-sacrifice, in response to which discomfort sets in or threatens, which calls for pharmacologic relief. In other words, taking drugs is not rationalized on pleasure-seeking grounds as is the case with marihuana, but on the grounds of offering a reward for enduring stress. These kind of rationalizations find few challenges, for other people tend to sympathize with them, whereas the attempts of pleasure-seeking youth to justify marihuana use meet with very little sympathy.

The drug effects usually are self-defeating. As a person finds and uses excuses for taking the drugs, he thereby avoids the opportunity to learn other ways of coping with stress or strain. This circumstance then creates the notion that drugs are a necessity, and thus the seed of drug abuse is sown.

The people who have been most heavily involved in this kind of drug sub-culture have been the housewives of the post-1955 period. Today's marihuana sub-culture is made up, to a major extent, of the children of these mothers. The influence of the one on the other is obvious, and it is interesting to note that the rebellious quality found in the marihuana culture takes the forms, not of being anti-establishment through being anti-drug (which would be a rather mature form of rebellion) but through finding anti-establishment excuses for making the same mistakes.

No taint of illegality has been directed toward the extensive use of, or prescribing for, the tranquilizers, although finding these drugs in the possession of someone not authorized to use them because he has no prescription is technically illegal. Since the drugs are rather easy to obtain, they enter the blackmarket freely.

ESOTERIC DRUG CULTURES

Beginning with LSD, then peyote, and strongly influenced by extensive publicity concerning the alleged mysterious properties of such drugs, another cult has also emerged in the past seven or eight years. Although often identified as being addicted to the use of one in particular of these more esoteric substances, those people who experiment with their use seem to use as their basis of choice the quality of novelty itself. In other words, they tend to make use of any substance reported to have novel properties, and this includes various mixtures of drugs taken together. Many of these groups, and they seem to be associated in groups, appear to be made up of the most rebellious and daring of young people, the ones likely to find novel ways of getting into trouble no matter what the current fashions happen to be. They are also apt to be articulate, or even highly literate, and thus serve as eloquent spokesmen for their cult. In a sense, they often regard themselves as the leaders, the trend-setters, of a generation of people, mostly young, who advocate the abolition of many old prohibitions, such as those directed against homosexuality, for instance, The causes they advocate do not serve to endear them to conventional society, however. With the attitude of finding through unusual drugs new, and exciting experiences, a setting becomes established for producing precisely these effects. Detailed study of some of these people demonstrates that their proclivity for fantasy and novelty leads them to interpret many commonplace experiences in a similar light—in other words, they tend to find something original, something dramatic, in many experiences—and so, it is no wonder that they appear to get the same kind of effects from drugs. The term "psychedelic" has been coined to refer to the drugs, the type of experiences, even to the interior decoration and music contrived to provide a proper setting for their use. The general tendency of these people to approach these experiences, and these drugs, with reckless abandon, rather than to consider the actual effects of the drugs themselves, makes these cultish practices assume dangerous proportions. The extensive resourcefulness of the sub-population involved, however, is sufficient to outwit any effort on the part of society to stamp them out.

THE SO-CALLED STIMULANTS

The relatively new category of drugs commonly known as stimulants (amphetamines) have acquired an unusual quasi-respectable aspect. They have been largely promoted by drug companies as having the capacity both to allay appetite (therefore ostensibly useful as aids in weight reduction) and to increase the level of alertness. Therefore, they have been freely prescribed by physicians for dieting or for helping people stay awake when they might otherwise be drowsy. Both of these objectives have acquired unusually high status, since losing weight is made to appear noble because it is supposedly a health measure, and help in staying awake is enobled in response to the alleged heavy demands on one to work. Thus, students take them to stay awake in order to study for exams, and truck drivers use them heavily to keep from falling asleep on the highway. The counter argument that they might also be damaging to health is outweighed by the nobility of such purposes. By extending these uses, then, certain groups of both young and not-so-young people have taken them intravenously.

Although the distribution of these drugs is apparently under drug control laws, and is limited to licensed pharmacists and physicians' prescriptions, there appears to be no difficulty finding a ready supply of them. It has been estimated that only about 25 percent of these drugs manufactured are actually distributed through legal prescriptions, the remainder somehow finding other channels of distribution. It is not unusual for people who have taken these drugs for their expected stimulating properties to end up in hospitals in rather serious states of toxicity.

There seems to be some tendency for those who use these drugs on a more or less regular basis at "speed" parties to regard themselves as somewhat superior to those in the marihuana culture. A kind of aristocracy of drug use thereby becomes established. A fairly sizable number of these people who have been studied indicates that they are fairly well-educated, intelligent, middle-class, but rather neurotic. Their drug use is often found to color adolescent adventures not unlike older days when bootleg liquor lubricated the antics of college boys. The most recent advice from groups known to the author indicates that experimentation with various mixtures is currently in fashion, and old-fashioned beer is said to be in the process of being rediscovered. Hospital admissions from auto accidents commonly disclose an antecedent admixture of drug effect with driving adventures, often with disastrous consequences.

7

DRUG EFFECTS
AND MYTHOLOGIES

CONCEPTS OF NARCOTIC ADDICTION

A SALIENT feature to be aware of in appraising the common attitudes about narcotic addiction is the inescapable fact that the theories that have evolved originated with the addicts themselves. This fact alone should be enough to lead an investigator looking for valid concepts in other directions to find the truth.

The basic traditional concept involves what constitutes addiction itself. The drug user's persistent demands for his drug, his enforcement of these demands with dire predictions and threats if they are not satisfied, and his occasionally dramatic reaction when he is denied his dosage constitute the evidence on which the concept has been built and largely accepted by physicians as well as the general public. To those who have had experience in treating so-called addicts, it becomes evident that these kinds of reactions are likely to be very prominent in those who are taken off drugs, but may be inconspicuous or absent in those who are highly motivated to give up drugs by themselves. In any event, it is these kinds of reactions that have led to the theory that certain people "need" the drug, that these persons are "dependent" on the drug. Hence, the phenomenon of drug addiction (the older term) or drug dependence.

The concept of addiction as it developed from observing the reactions of certain persons to threats of being denied drugs leads to the assumption that, in certain people, the administration of a narcotic drug (the prototype being morphine) on one occasion establishes in that person some kind of sensitivity, or dependency. After his first

MARIHUANA AND THE WORLD OF YOUTH

"Marihuana has become both a focus and a symbol of the generation gap and for many young people its use has become an expedient means of protest against adult values.

"Adults in positions of authority, parents, teachers, police officials, judges, and others often view marihuana use as the sign of youth's rejection of moral and social values and of the system of government under which they live. The problem is that both youth and adults tend to make pronouncements and are frequently unable to reason together in logical fashion. Instead they overstate their positions in such a way that effective resolution of their differences becomes very difficult."

Marihuana: a Signal of Misunderstanding, *First Report of the National Commission on Marihuana and Drug Abuse, March, 1972, U.S. Government Printing Office.*

exposure, he will develop a biochemical need for drugs such that failure to obtain repeated doses results in an altered physiological state that stimulates an "uncontrollable craving." Failure to satisfy this craving leads him into a state of serious physiological disequilibrium or impels him to adopt desperate measures to satisfy his need. In other words, the physiological state that allegedly is created once the person is sensitized by exposure to the drug is described as being comparable to the situation of diabetics whose physiological state is such that they need continuous doses of insulin in order to maintain a desirable physiological equilibrium. However, people who are diabetic or vitamin deficient do not develop any craving for any particular biochemical, even though they may need it. The severe diabetic, for instance, may easily find himself in a situation in which his very life may depend on a dose of insulin, but he develops no craving for insulin. He is much more likely to crave candy, which is forbidden him because it will make his condition worse.

A principal reason for supposing that once the need for a narcotic drug develops in a person a new physiological state is created that requires constant replenishment of the drug is what is called the "withdrawal" syndrome. In a few cases, when the addicting drug is withdrawn, within a few hours to a few days, what looks like a physiological collapse sets in. This state, it is alleged, stems from the fact that the biochemical need is not being satisfied, thus leaving the subject in a state of physiological disequilibrium. This state is, then, allegedly corrected by administering the drug in question, thus supposedly meeting this need. To ward off the onset of these states, it is not unusual for drug termination programs to emphasize gradual diminution in dosage over a long period of time. Thus, according to this concept, the person is gradually desensi-

MARIHUANA EFFECTS: DIFFERING VIEWPOINTS

1. "The most consistently striking finding in all these studies is that marihuana produced no striking findings. Indeed, one is impressed with how easily subjects could suppress the marihuana 'high.'"

The Marijuana Problem, *Norman Q. Brill, M.D.,* Annals of Internal Medicine, *1970.*

2. "Marijuana, unlike opium, is an excitant drug. It disrupts and destroys the brain and distorts the mind, resulting in crime and degeneracy. It attacks the central nervous system and violently affects the mentality and five physical senses. Time, space and distance are obliterated, and hallucinations occur. Marijuana, like cocaine, is the immediate and direct cause of the crime committed."

Narcotics and Hallucinogenics: A Handbook, *J. B. Williams, editor, 1967, the Glencoe Press.*

tized to the need. Furthermore, according to this theory, the person who has thus been terminated will become almost immediately and almost invariably resensitized to the need if exposed to another dose.

It has been further postulated that the phenomenon of addiction is one to which only a small percentage of a population is vulnerable. Given a large number of unselected people who have been given, medically, a dose of morphine, only a small percentage of them will go on to become addicts. In this respect, then, the phenomenon of addiction is similar to drinking wherein many people become exposed to alcohol use, but only a small percentage end up as alcoholics.

In addition to the similarity with alcohol, other kinds of human behavior fit into the same class—namely, a situation to which some people respond moderately and rationally whereas others respond destructively. Other rather obvious examples would be the way in which people (rational or otherwise) use other, non-narcotic drugs such as aspirin, common sedatives, or even laxatives. Somewhat more removed, but still having a chemical underpinning, would be drinking coffee and tea or smoking tobacco. Still further removed, and having much in common in terms of effects on life and health, but having little or no chemical denominators, would be overeating, gambling, klepto-

POETRY OF THE MARIHUANA CULT

". . . from habitual shallow, purely verbal guidelines and repetitive secondhand ideological interpretations of experience to more direct, slower, absorbing, occasionally microscopically minute, engagement with sensing phenomena during the high moments after one has smoked . . ." (describing the pre-drug state to the drug state transition).

From Allen Ginsberg, The Atlantic Monthly, *November, 1966.*

mania, and other unique neurotic compulsions. A scale of addictions might be devised from these theories ranking the corresponding behaviors according to progressively less degrees of malignancy.

Addictive behaviors with progressively less degree of malignancy:

1. Heroin or morphine addiction
2. Addiction to the synthetic analgesics (demerol)
3. Alcoholism
4. Codeine addiction
5. Marihuana, amphetamine, barbituate, tranquilizer addiction
6. Aspirin, etc. habit
7. Coffee, tea, tobacco habit
8. Compulsive gambling, compulsive stealing
9. Over-eating
10. Essentially harmless compulsive habits

INROADS INTO TRADITIONAL CONCEPTS

The simplified and original concept of addiction served its purpose adequately until more careful studies were made of the phenomenon. Both clinical and psychological investigations of so-called addicts, as well as the continuous discovery of wider and wider populations of people who came to be included under the concept, brought about modifications of the theory. Faith in the original theory, however, is still strongly and widely maintained, so that modifications that came to be accepted tended to be more or less consistent with the original. A major, unresolved, but generally unrecognized dilemma was encountered, on the other hand. The original concept stressed the idea that the unique factors responsible for addiction resided in certain people, but not others, and

BAUDELAIRE'S DESCRIPTION OF THE EFFECTS OF MARIHUANA (CIRCA 1850)

". . . the senses become extraordinarily acute and fine. The eyes pierce Infinity. The ear perceives the most imperceptible in the midst of the sharpest noises. Hallucinations begin. External objects take on monstrous appearances and reveal themselves under forms hitherto unknown. They then become deformed as at last they enter into your being or rather you enter into theirs. The most singular equivocations, the most inexplicable transposition of ideas takes place. Sounds have odor and colors are musical. . . . After a first stage of hysterical laughter and crying, the second state is characterized by a sensation of weakness in the extremities and heaviness of the head. The hands tremble, there is a general stupefaction, the eyes become large, the face pales and then grows livid and greenish."

From Lester Grinspoon, Marihuana Reconsidered *(Cambridge: Harvard University Press, 1971). The author goes on to describe Baudelaire's experimentation with alcohol, opium, and hashish. This period of Baudelaire's life coincided with his joining a Bohemian literary culture in Paris, contributing a substantial precedent for the subsequent association of drugs and poetry.*

only certain people with these unspecified characteristics would likely become addicted. Within the framework of this concept, it then seemed logical that addiction could be abolished if morphine and its derivatives could be abolished. This, conceivably, could be accomplished by developing new, synthetic drugs having very different chemical properties, but having the medically desired analgesic properties of morphine. Under the sponsorship of the Committee on Narcotics and Drug Addiction of the National Research Council, research was launched to discover such a drug. This effort was greatly stimulated during World War II when it seemed likely that supplies of opium, the raw materials used in making morphine, would be cut off. The research was successful, pharmacologically. A new synthetic drug, demerol, was discovered, which had the desired analgesic properties and which was also distinctly different chemically from morphine. According to the old theory, then, as this new drug was substituted for morphine in medicine, the creation of new narcotic addicts would be substantially reduced. In very short order, however, certain people became "addicted" to demerol in the same way that others had become addicted to morphine. After demerol, more and more analgesic, sedative, and "tranquilizing" drugs were discovered to have the same effect, and other like drugs are still being discovered. An interesting phenomenon now apparent is that new drugs of this sort have to be available for some time before cases of abuse become known.

The rather abrupt discovery that many different chemical substances can be addicting, then led to a new concept; namely, that there exists not only an "addictive potential" in certain people, but also an "addictive potential" in certain drugs. The widely different chemical make-up of these drugs made it increasingly difficult to justify the unique biochemical phenomenon that addiction was supposed to be. A new modification of the theory then appeared, which alleged that there were different degrees of addiction. These degrees were supposed to range from the more serious one of old-fashioned addiction to a milder form of "habituation." Drugs were then said to be either addictive or habit forming. Ostensibly, then, habit-forming drugs could be terminated in much the same way as breaking a tobacco-smoking habit.

Further experience with drug users has more recently led to the "discovery" that some people who were apparently addicts could stop taking drugs at will, and that this happened with a previously unsuspected degree of frequency. Also, some people took their addicting drugs only sporadically, with no apparently ill effects during periods of abstinence. This apparent contradiction of the old theory brought about another modification, although the basic concept still remained. The new development proposed two types of drug abuse, one a "physiological dependence," which presumed that the unique properties of addiction were common only to a small number of addicts, the other a "psychological dependence," which stressed that others found a need for drugs only under certain variable psychological conditions. Those cases that did not conform to the old theory thus were split off and the theory was preserved. According to the modification, a given person might be either (1) physiologically and psychologically dependent, or (2) only psychologically dependent.

One of the pieces of evidence that was used to justify the old concept was the phenomenon of so-called "tolerance." A given subject sometimes steadily increases his daily dosage required to maintain his dependence. Before narcotic users were extensively studied, it was generally assumed that this phenomenon was the rule rather than the exception and was indicative of a growing tolerance of the body to the drug. After more careful studies got under way, however, it was found that, not only did this not invariably happen, but many of the people in which it did appear to happen were actually being victimized by increasing dilutions of the drug they obtained on the blackmarket, creating an illusion of increasing need. Physicians, too, who were administering narcotics to users would commonly attempt to wean them off the drug by secretly administering diluted doses—but creating in the user's mind the notion that he was taking larger and larger doses, or that the old dose no longer had the same effect. Again, the concept of tolerance was derived largely from the distortions of the narcotic user himself. Even alcoholics are typically subjected to diluted doses by bartenders who either are trying to victimize them, or trying to reduce their intake. In hospitals, it has not been at all uncommon for non-physician personnel to administer diluted doses as a way of acquiring a supply for themselves, but creating an impression that the subject is becoming tolerant.

The subject who is apparently dependent solely on psychological grounds is the kind who appears to demand his drug only during periods of psychological stress, and in whom withdrawal is manifested by a confrontation with this stress. His being able to "turn on" or "turn off" his drug use, or even to find substitutes that seem to serve the same psychological purpose, dealt a devastating blow to the concept of physiological dependence, but the concept was protected by inventing this separate category. Another observation that had a similar effect on the concept is the well-known fact that the particular drug in most widespread use tends to depend on the local availability, so that major shifts in the demand occur as supply changes. The ability of an addict to shift from one drug to another violated the old concept. Partially, these observations have been integrated into the theories, however, by postulating that some, or all, abusers of drugs escalate their use from the relatively more benign (alcohol, marihuana) to the more malignant (heroin). The fact, however, that frequently the opposite happens is not easily rationalized.

CHALLENGES TO THE OLD
CONCEPTS

If the theories that have evolved, and that are widely accepted, were subjected to a total re-evaluation in the light of the knowledge now available, their credibility would be seriously impaired. Some of the fundamental challenges that have not been directed at the concepts might be examined, as follows:

1. Investigators who have made intensive studies of the characterology of so-called drug addicts tend to be impressed by the personality structures of these people, and find it much more feasible to link these qualities with their abuse of drugs than to look for biochemical explanations. They find, for instance, that these people typically engage in various kinds of behavior in the same excessive, self-defeating ways that they take to drugs. It is not uncommon, for instance, to find that they are compulsive gamblers, or that they shift freely from excessive and unreasonable use of drugs other than narcotics, including alcohol. The common allegation that their craving makes them so desperate that they will "resort to anything," such as criminal acts, to finance their habit is placed in a different light when one finds how difficult it is to get them to go to work for a living, a means by which they could accomplish these ends without risking arrest. In other words, it is exceedingly rare to find a heroin addict desperate enough to go to work. On the other hand, another class of drug abusers, those who take up the use of nar-

cotics secondary to their exposure to them through working as physicians, nurses, and in other similar capacities
find that hospital employment offers a good source of drug
supplies, and hold on to their jobs. The typical, long-
standing, "hard-core" addicts invariably demonstrate a
life-long commitment to avoiding responsibility. The
search for the easy way to obtain gratifications is characteristic of their entire approach to life. They tend to be
passive, dependent, with little thought given to long-term
planning and are generally fearful of any kind of discomfort or threat of inconvenience. It is from these kinds of
people that emanate the insistent demands for repeated
drug dosages, a phenomenon that creates the concept of
craving.

Comparative studies of marihuana users and heroin
users usually show a characterological difference, with
the former being less likely to elect the very extreme irresponsible route. Marihuana users, but not heroin users,
typically plan ahead enough to build up a stockpile of
supplies sufficient to last them a month or so, whereas the
heroin user typically manages his supply on a day-to-day
basis. This difference is probably responsible more than
anything else for the observation that the marihuana habit
is much less malignant than heroin addiction, although the
credit is more often given the drug than to the user. The
heroin user exposes himself to arrest almost daily as he
obtains his supply, whereas the marihuana user reduces
his arrest liability by exposing himself to the law only
once a month or so; thus, the heroin addict appears to
be more involved in criminal activity.

2. The phenomenon of withdrawal is another fundamental piece of evidence in support of the traditional
theory. The fact that it does not invariably occur when
a narcotic user is taken off his drug should be enough to

discredit the evidence. Over and over again, the dramatic withdrawal syndrome frequently portrayed in movies and on television occurs most commonly under the following circumstances: (a) when the user is being forcibly, or coercively, rather than willingly and cooperatively, taken off the drug. Under these kind of psychological circumstances, it is no surprise that the subject exhibits the most violent type of protest. (b) Also, the most uncomfortable and distressing reactions occur in those users who have been victims of various complications issuing from drug use—such as toxicity from the drug itself, infection from unclean instruments used to inject drugs, long periods of poor nutrition, and so on. In most, if not all, instances, the unfortunate reactions can be ascribed more accurately to these combinations of complications than to the mere abstinence from the drug in question. The fact that during these periods the user resorts to his usual mode of coping with discomfort by demanding the drug is what has led so many people to think that abstinence was the cause of the difficulty.

3. Another common observation that contains a fundamental contradiction not generally recognized as such is connected with withdrawal. A common way (often used, for instance, at the Lexington, Kentucky USPHS Hospital) of detoxifying a user is to place him on a regime of gradually decreasing doses of the drug, perhaps finally shifting to another, non-narcotic drug, then ending the treatment. This method allegedly results in a gradual desensitizing effect. However, later on, a single exposure to another dose immediately "re-sensitizes" the subject and his addiction is thus restored. The contradiction mentioned is embodied in the following observation. If, on June 1, the final dose in the detoxifying program is administered, and this dose is one-eighth of a grain, this dose is considered

to be a therapeutic dose, which can effectively wean the
subject from use of the drug. If, however, on July 1, that
same dose is repeated, then the whole addiction process
starts all over again. The question is, How can a certain
dose of a given drug on one day have the opposite effect
of the same dose of the same drug on some other day?
Obviously, the drug cannot have two different, opposite
effects on the same person at different times. However, a
more rational explanation, which conforms quite closely
with what is observed characterologically about these drug
users, is that on June 1, the subject was prepared, psychologically, to give up his drug taking, but by July 1, he
had (typically, and short-sightedly) changed his mind and
had every intention of returning to the drug.

Medical personnel (doctors, nurses) who become narcotic abusers characteristically obtain access to pure, high-
grade narcotics and usually manage to find ways of maintaining their supply with little risk of arrest. These people
seldom escalate their dosage (because their drug is not
being subject to dilution?) and rarely experience any of
the dramatic withdrawal effects (minimum of toxic complications). These observations are further probable indi-
cations that the other subjects who experience serious
withdrawal symptoms are actually suffering from toxicity
and other complications rather than from abstinence per
se.

4. Another serious challenge to the old theories could
be presented as a rhetorical question: Why is it that so-
called addiction involves *only* chemicals that are used by
people who think they produce comfort or pleasure? Why
is not turpentine, for instance, addicting? Why is it that
the pleasurable or comfort-producing properties have to
be "discovered" before a drug problem is created, even
though the drug might have been around and in use for

a long time? For instance, some of the so-called tranquilizers were formerly sold and widely used as antihistamines
for hay fever but did not become problem drugs until
they were found to be effective in "relieving anxiety." According to the old concepts, which were based on an
alleged biochemical phenomenon in the body's reaction to
the drug, it would be consistent if a list of chemicals having very similar chemical properties, but not necessarily
common psychological effects, were addicting. The opposite, instead, has been true. Many similar chemicals but
with different psychological effects are available, and only
the ones thought to be pleasurable or comfort-producing
become problems. Many chemically different substances
producing the same psychological effects also are problem
drugs. It is also true that the degree of so-called "addiction liability" is merely a function of how effective the
drugs are as analgesics and in terms of other properties.
Therefore, morphine is much more "liable" than codeine,
even though they are similar chemically, but the former
is a much more potent analgesic than the latter. In other
words, it is clearly evident that it is the psychological
effect that is sought by drug abusers, not a biochemical
effect; and a not inconsiderable factor in producing the
desired psychological effect is a culturally determined one
that defines it as "pleasant." These cultural determinants
have even been known to fall into disrepute; "laughing
gas" parties in the mid-nineteenth century lost their popularity, for instance.

5. The kind of subjects with which physicians in the
past have usually had the most experience were their patients who claimed to have some source of serious discomfort, usually pain, and usually of a chronic or recurring
nature. These patients have been typically those who made
extravagantly neurotic demands for relief from their symp-

toms, and who characteristically faced a recurrence of
these symptoms with great anxiety. Such patients tend to
accept almost any kind of treatment measure that promises them some sort of relief, and, therefore, frequently
become the victims of repeated surgical operations. Since,
however, the most significant aspect of the problem is not,
as the physician usually thinks, the pain complained of,
but the anxiety experienced in anticipating its reappear-
ance, any treatment measure employed is likely to have
only temporary benefits. Sooner or later, such patients are
likely to be given a dose of narcotic, and the effective
analgesic properties of the opiates tends to create in these
people the conviction that they have finally found the in-
stant relief they have been seeking, thus becoming addicts.
Thereafter, these patients are likely to shop around among
physicians, as one after another tries, unsuccessfully and
perhaps with some guilt, to wean them off the drug. The
evident anxiety these people experience when they anticipate having to face a recurrence of their painful symptoms
without a narcotic supply on hand to help them is easily
misconstrued as an addict's "craving for the drug." These
people represent that group whose drug use is negatively
motivated, that is, they are anxiously seeking protection
from the occurrence of painful symptoms.

There is another group of drug abusers, however, with
whom physicians have not had so much experience because
their introduction to drugs has come through non-medical
channels and because they rely on the blackmarket for
their supply. These people are usually introduced to drugs,
and continue to take them in order to find pleasure, a
pleasure that they learn from the drug culture. These people are not particularly concerned about having to do
without drugs; rather, they look forward to getting them,
but are not necessarily anxious or disappointed if they do

not. They do not exhibit the classic craving symptoms, particularly when they begin taking drugs. Unfortunately, however, they sometimes come to rely solely on drugs for pleasure, and then the prospects of being without a supply leads them to expect that a kind of emptiness and loneliness will overtake them, which motivates them strongly to do something about it.

Today, perhaps for the first time on the American scene (but perhaps very common in other cultures), an increasing number of rather ordinary people experiment with drugs a few times, or infrequently, for the sake of the expected pleasure and social excitement. As these practices become more and more common, and in certain fairly respectable but somewhat unconventional circles, more and more fairly mature and reasonable people join these groups. The current trends indicate that certain kinds of drug use will soon take on a status comparable to social drinking. Under the old concepts, this fashion would have seemed inconceivable, for no reasonable, responsible person would have been expected to use these drugs deliberately unless they were medically prescribed, and then only rarely. In other words, the old concepts looked upon drug abuse much as many of the old temperance advocates saw drinking—namely, any kind of experimenting would surely lead to ruination, and yielding to the temptation was already proof of a "weak character."

The point of these latter observations is to indicate that the parallels between drug use and alcohol use are becoming obviously more marked than the differences. In both cases, it is now becoming evident, it is the psychological characteristics of people, as measured by their degrees of maturity and common sense, which distinguishes the rational user from the addict.

NEW CONCEPTS OF DRUG ABUSE

In keeping with a new, liberalized viewpoint, which has grown out of more objective, less moralistic, studies of drug users, the term "addiction" with all of its theoretical implications is falling by the wayside, to be replaced by the expression "drug abuse." The popular press and law enforcement spokesmen continue, as always, to follow the old, obsolete terminology and concepts. The newer concepts differ from the old, not only in fundamental philosophy, but also in degree of complexity, and this second factor becomes an obstacle to introducing them to a wide audience. The degree of complexity is the inevitable outgrowth of any study of widespread human behaviors in which many different kinds of people, with many different kinds of motivations, have some single practice in common (e.g., drug use, voting Republican, being poor, engaging in crime, etc.). Society in general, newspaper people and law enforcement officials in particular, eternally seek to find universal laws of human behavior that will explain in simple, cause-and-effect terms, how and why people do what they do. But what they fail to realize is that different kinds of people end up doing the same things but for widely different reasons, because the choices that *appear to be* (implying that what appears to be is often much more limited than what is really so) available to people are much fewer than the number of different motivations available. A case in point is the choice of candidates for president, wherein only two choices are apparently available but the reasons for making a choice may go into the hundreds. The *apparent* choices are dictated to a large degree by fashions. A new fashion tends to attract a certain class of citizen with certain, rather discrete sets of characteristics, one of which is likely to be unconventionality. But once the fashion becomes established, more conventionally minded people tend to go along with it.

In any event, a theory of drug use, if it is to be more rational than the traditional one, must allow for much greater diversity. To be credible, it must recognize the striking similarities that exist between the use of drugs and the use of alcohol, and it must further recognize the role of legal prohibition itself as one of the variables, which although designed to solve a problem may, in fact, be instrumental in causing a problem. The latter observation was quite applicable to alcohol use and liquor prohibition during the twenties. This applicability is usually understandable to most thoughtful people, but few of them today see the striking parallels with today's drug prohibition. Furthermore, theories of drug use must take into account two separate sets of problems that may not be at all amenable to treatment within the same theory. One of these sets of problems might be called the "personal problem" area, which has to do with the self-destructive use of excessive and dangerous drugs as this practice is related to the drug user's own personal problems. The other set might be referred to as the "social problem" area, which has to do with questions of drug traffic, disrespect for the law, organized crime, drug cultures, and the like.

Some of the elements of a new viewpoint on drug use that takes account of the many variations in the problem would include the following:

1. Although it is likely to be an unpopular observation in many conventional circles of society, it has now become quite apparent that the various drugs capable of destructive or irrational use are being, and will probably continue to be used, for apparently rational purposes by fairly responsible and rational people. In other words, as al-

ready alluded to, all the psychoactive drugs will have to
be placed in the same class with alcoholic beverages in
the sense that, just as "normal social drinking" takes place
frequently, "normal drug use" will also have to be recognized as a reality. Not any property of the drugs themselves, but rather certain culturally defined social
institutions have permitted this situation to develop. These
institutions have been, like cocktail parties, newly invented
social customs in which the normal purpose of friendship
and pleasure motivated groups of people to share a common experience in which, incidentally, drug use occurred.
As with the cocktail party, the same social purpose could
be fulfilled without the chemical lubricant, but the chemical serves as a kind of excuse, a kind of justification for
achieving a level of intimacy among members of a group
that conventional protocol ordinarily does not permit.
Rather than attacking this excuse, it would be wiser to
examine, with a view toward change, those social customs
that place such unusual restraints on people's enjoying
one another's company without these excuses. As civilization becomes characterized by denser concentrations of
people, then greater care is exercised by people in protecting their privacy. As this tendency progresses, the various
customs and protocols of politeness that develop to govern
society tend to erect barriers against a free interchange
of pleasurable experiences. As a consequence, pleasure and
friendship tend to become increasingly institutionalized.
In this setting, then, a greater rather than lesser need
arises to find excuses for being intimate; hence, the drug
and drinking rituals surrounding social occasions. In short,
drug use itself cannot be considered as invariably a problem.

2. In addition to that class of drug users comparable
to rational drinkers of alcohol, whose use does not appear

to constitute a problem, there are, of course, other kinds of people whose use of drugs does generate problems. The difference between the two groups of people, then, is much like the difference in people who practice either constructively or destructively any other human behavior—such as driving an automobile safely or unsafely, eating food in a reasonable way or over-eating, taking to religion in a moderate as opposed to a "fanatical" way, and so on. Clearly, people who abuse rather than use anything constructively are inclined to be people with immature levels of judgment, a quality that leads them to make immature decisions about many life situations, including the way in which they use drugs or alcohol. The fact that some drug abusers, for instance, prefer to steal instead of work in order to earn money to "support the habit" is one of these manifestations. A new light is shed on drug abuse when we regard it as irrational behavior prompted by immature judgments. It becomes, then, instead of something that happens to a given person, or something that a person does, something that has not happened, something he does not do. It is a problem, in a sense, by default. The appropriate question to ask, from this viewpoint, is not "Why does this individual use drugs destructively?" but "Why does he not use them rationally, like other (rational) people do?" In other words, the drug abuser is not one who "has" something other people do not have (e.g., addiction potential), but, rather, he does not have what others do have. He does not have the maturity, the level of judgment, other people have that leads them to make constructive decisions in life. Judgment of a high quality, at a mature level, is something people have to learn through long experience and exposure to good models. Some people do not acquire sound judgment because they have not had the necessary experience. Thus, children have immature judgment and cannot be trusted to use alcohol or drugs rationally. Many adolescents and adults are in the same class because they have not progressed beyond a child's degree of maturity.

A convincing argument in favor of this viewpoint toward both drug and alcohol abuse comes from studies of people who have successfully grown from immature to mature adults. This very often happens, sometimes with the help of professional guidance, but also without such help. These people, once they have "grown up," begin to exercise sounder judgement in managing their lives, and they give up irrational ways of using drugs or alcohol. They may then continue to use the chemicals in a more rational way, or not use them at all. The frequency with which this happens is borne out by the observation that both alcohol and drug abuse decline with age. Clearly, the people who have made these changes have not changed their biochemistry—they have only improved their way of making decisions.

3. Within that group of immature people who use drugs and alcohol with the same poor judgment that they apply to other aspects of their lives, there are at least two major groups that can be classified according to the general type of motivation involved. All people can be said to do some things with negative motivations and other things with positive motivations. The negative ones are those in which some activity is performed in order to prevent something undesirable from happening (e.g., buying insurance), whereas the positive ones are performed, hopefully at least, in order to achieve something desirable (e.g., buying a car in order to have transportation to work). Immature people are also both positively and negatively motivated. That group of immature people known as neurotics are apt to do a great many things in life for negative reasons

(in order to avoid something). The kind of people to whom psychiatrists attach the label "personality disorder" are likely to be characterized by a tendency to do many impulsive, poorly thought-out things for the sake of finding personal pleasure or other gratifications. Thus, in connection with the decisions these people might make about the use of drugs or alcohol, one group is likely to abuse chemicals with the idea or expectation that the chemical effect will protect them against something undesirable (e.g., pain, anxiety, boredom, loneliness, and so on). The other group, on the other hand, would be more likely to be positively motivated and to seek pleasure through use of these chemicals. This difference adequately accounts for the differences found in the so-called craving in drug abusers, for when it is something dreaded that the person seeks to protect himself from by using drugs or drink, then the search for a new dose is accompanied by incipient panic. The other kind of person, however, acts toward an obstacle to his next dose as an impulsive, immature person would toward any frustration of his pleasure—with belligerence in some cases, by conniving in others, or with indifference in still others. The threat of denying this person sexual pleasure, for instance, would likely elicit the same responses.

4. Another factor of great importance in understanding the way in which immature people handle drugs or alcohol can be seen in the typical ways in which they handle other life situations. Much of what they do tends to be self-defeating—that is to say, the ends they seek are defeated by the means they use. The neurotic, for instance, typically uses various avoidance maneuvers in order to protect himself from unpleasant consequences, but, in so doing, becomes exposed to either the very unpleasant results feared or some other undesired outcome. The other

kind of person who tends to operate at an impulsive,
short-sighted, pleasure-seeking level also ends up with
very unpleasurable results—such as being arrested or experiencing undesirable drug effects, or being tyrannized
by those on whom they have made themselves dependent.
In other words, one of the qualities of these people that
so distorted the old theories was the fact that the ends
gained were not the ends sought; but the old theories
assumed that the ends gained must have been the ends
sought. Drug abusers become dependent on drugs not because of some inherent property in the drugs, but because
these people came to rely solely on a single route for
gaining satisfactions to the exclusion of all others, a quality
that is eminently characteristic of people who employ
self-defeating methods. Their readiness to rely on drugs
or alcohol, a reliance that excluded other alternatives, is
determined largely by the fact that the chemicals seem
to give the pleasure or the comfort they seek with a minimum of responsibility, and, above all, without the necessity that mature people accept of waiting for rewards. By
"putting all their eggs in one basket," so to speak, they
sometimes experience a sense of desperation over the
prospects of losing what they have come to rely on. Other
people can "take or leave" drugs or alcohol because they
have developed many sources of satisfaction, so that no
single one appears to be critical.

5. In addition to the group of people who could be
considered to use drugs (and alcohol) in a fairly rational,
non-destructive way, and the group that carries their use
to extremes because of their immature ways of behaving,
thinking, and handling responsibility, still another group
must be considered. This is the large group of adolescent
"thrill-seekers" who briefly experiment with a nondescript
list of drugs, but most often marihuana. These people, too,

are characterized by a less than optimum level of maturity, but still perhaps are no more immature than might be expected of any group of adolescents. The combination of some degree of rebelliousness against convention, misconstrued as independence, and a healthy search for new grown-up experiences is likely to lead these young people into any number of fairly risky experiences—with members of the opposite sex, with automobiles, with money, and with drugs and alcohol. Typically, these adolescents learn to moderate their behavior after having such experiences, and most go on to become adults who live quite conventional lives. These are the people for whom the legal prohibitions represent a special, double-barreled threat. On the one hand, they tend to be attracted to the romanticized drug culture *because* it is forbidden (therefore, in the adolescent mind, adult and desirable). On the other hand, experimentation becomes a threat because of the possibility of their naïveté getting them arrested, thus casting a serious blot on their budding careers.

Conventional society has, apparently since the beginning of its creation, made the mistake of assuming that strict prohibitions against engaging in potentially dangerous activities must be enforced against adolescents in order to protect them from the experimentation that adolescents are prone to engage in. Hence, smoking, sex, and drinking, are sternly forbidden in youth, but not in adulthood. This kind of discrimination, however, has always served the contrary purpose of labeling these activities as desirable and has only attracted youth to engage in them. If, instead, it were forbidden youth to study enlightened literature, to work hard, or to show consideration for other people, perhaps these activities could acquire a degree of popularity they have never known. Instead, society converts them into obligations. Almost by definition, then, an obligation is something to reduce to a minimum and prohibited activities are those that must be pursued at all cost, thus creating the attitudes precisely opposite to what society intends. Drugs enter into this age-old picture because of current fashions, which, like others, might soon pass away—but when and if that happens, it will be because something else has taken their place. From responsible people in positions of leadership must come substitute activities (and perhaps the most feasible way to begin is to declare them forbidden). Some examples might be: campaigning for political candidates, boycotting businesses that contribute to air and water pollution, learning Chinese, learning difficult occupational skills, playing chess, walking instead of riding in cars, spending summers working on farms, or a host of others.

6. Another major factor in involving some people in drug abuse is the very respectable and almost universal belief in the efficacy of drugs as a way of solving problems. A major step in bringing about this state of affairs has been the recent extension of medical responsibility to include concern for an interest in the morale problems of patients who seek medical attention. The siege of physicians' offices by complaining, unhappy people in perfectly good health had always been a problem, and the typical physician of the past felt quite uncomfortable in handling them. With the advent of the tranquilizers, and the expert promotional campaign that made their alleged magical properties a part of American folklore, physicians were given not only a way out of an old dilemma, but also something in which they developed a great deal of confidence. Nothing has as great a placebo effect as a willing patient who fully expects to get relief from a pill prescribed by a physician who exudes confidence in its curative powers. This is why these pills work now, today, and did not work in the past, even though they were available, for then neither patient nor

physician felt any confidence in them. The fiction now is so pervasive that it is not at all uncommon today to find physicians (or clinics, or hospitals) who regard it as a cure when a patient is taken off one drug he is abusing and put on another that he also abuses. Hence, the great faith in the methadone method of treating heroin addiction. Alcoholics, for instance, regularly have their tastes shifted from alcohol to tranquilizers and end up with the same results, although convinced that a great improvement has occurred.

Up to this point, I have avoided discussing some terms because they contribute very little of a conceptual character to the subject, having been employed largely for jurisdictional purposes only. I refer particularly to the term "sickness" as it has been applied to those people who have carried to an extreme and irrational level the use of drugs or alcohol. The term probably originated with those alcoholics who became affiliated with Alcoholics Anonymous and was taken up by narcotics users who have been engaged in self-help projects such as Synanon. The frequent distress experienced by the abusers of various chemicals, such as the "hangovers," could have been enough to justify the term to some extent, although such phenomena are more in the nature of consequences than causes. More important, however, the term has been used to counter the allegations commonly made by legislators and law-enforcement people who have treated the victims of excessive drugs and alcohol as criminals. In other words, the term "sick" was largely designed as a more worthy substitute for what others prefer to call "criminal," and as such naturally appeals to the victims themselves. Eventually, as medical people began to take more responsibility for caring for the alcoholic and the drug abuser, physicians classified them as "sick" in the same way that they classify everybody else who comes to their attention. This is what a jurisdictional label means—a term used by physicians to stake out their territory at the expense of law-enforcement people who use different concepts.

When physicians call people "sick," very little if anything is implied by the classification except to indicate that physicians thereby recognize some responsibility for their care. This move has not been very popular in medical circles, nor one that has been strongly defended. In spite of the fact that physicians are, indeed, inclined to recognize a responsibility in the drug and alcohol problem, they do not generally find it very attractive, and very, very little is done about it. Medical societies or individual physicians are apt to admit the need to do more, but generally advocate that some public agency be the one to do it, meanwhile realizing that city, county, and state health agencies have an extraordinarily difficult time recruiting medical personnel for any kind of jobs, and even more difficulty in this unpopular area. Mostly, therefore, the various clinics or hospital services set up to provide medical care for alcohol and drug problems tend to be token affairs, or, at best, enjoy only a brief period of constructive activity, usually during the leadership of an occasional dedicated professional. Most professionals who have had experience in caring for these problems become sadly disillusioned over the poor cooperation they get from others, the indifferent results, and the general failure of the kind of people who inhabit the drug and drinking cultures to share with them the same sanctified attitude toward such middle-class values as keeping appointments, paying bills, and the like.

In certain sophisticated, intellectual circles, it is considered unusually humane and progressive to insist on the sick label for the drug abuser and alcoholic. This trend finds ready, popular support in the newspapers, movies, and television. Professional writers and entertainers tend to subscribe to this point of view, not only because of their tendency to align themselves with a liberal, intellectual viewpoint, but also because so many of their own members are victims of the problems in question.

In other words, the point of these remarks is to indicate that the sick label is a euphemism that places a kind of gloss on a major social problem that more conservative elements of society prefer to treat as a crime. A Supreme Court decision gave great credence to this euphemism when it ruled that the state of California could not treat any condition of one of its citizens, such as narcotics abuse, as a crime when the evidence indicated that the acquisition of a narcotic habit could not be assumed to have been done with criminal intent.

Although the sick and the criminal labels are frequently debated, the discussions add nothing to a conceptual (right or wrong) understanding of the issue. A crime, after all, is purely a matter of definition; that is to say, any activity prohibited by law is a crime. Before the law was placed on the statute books, of course, the same activity was not a crime, and if the law were repealed it would automatically cease being a crime. Because of this arbitrary nature of what constitutes a crime, debate at a theoretical level is meaningless.

In brief, it is important to the ultimate solution of the social problem of drugs and alcohol that the extensive mythology that enjoys general lay and professional respect be understood for what it is. A major fall-out from the prevailing myths is the very common ways in which efforts to deal with the problems are actually perpetuating them. Belief in unfounded and distorted concepts has been based on mere wishful thinking rather than on objective investigation. Too much of what is done to solve the problems has turned out to be nothing but the blocks that pave the road to Hell—that is, good intentions.

Chapter
8

THE NEW DRUG PROHIBITION

BACKGROUND

In this current period of the seventies, there is a rapidly growing awareness and a public alarm over the influence of the Orient on the use of drugs by Americans as our military men show increasing tendencies to both experiment and become addicted to drugs in Viet Nam. It is probably this new threat that has recently (1971) led the Nixon administration to launch new, large-scale programs in this country in an effort to cope with the internal problem. Many of the measures being advocated are those recommended in 1963 by the President's (Kennedy) Commission on Narcotics and Drug Abuse. The influence of the Orient in respect to the drug problem is not a new one. The British found, in the mid-nineteenth century, that opium from India was a useful instrument of trade with China, which exchanged silk and tea for the drug. The Opium Wars of the 1800s established British supremacy (The Treaty of Nanking, 1842) in this

opium trade, over the opposition of the Chinese government. The clipper-ship trade from the U.S. began, subsequently, to include opium as one of its most profitable
cargoes. The latter half of the nineteenth century, then,
was marked by an increasing availability and use of opium
preparations by the American public. The Michigan Board
of Health surveyed the state in 1877 because of its awareness that a problem already existed. The survey discovered
7,763 opium addicts in a population of 1.3 million. In one
small town (Adrian) of only 10,235 population, there were
11 addicts. By the early 1900s, there were 600,000 pounds
of opium per year being imported into the country.

OUTLINE OF THE BRITISH SYSTEM OF NARCOTIC CONTROL

1. The Dangerous Drug Act of 1920 provides the
legal basis.
2. Addicts are not regarded as criminals, there are
no legal sanctions against possession or use.
3. Physicians are permitted to prescribe narcotics
to users, they are urged to reduce dosage and attempt cure, and urged to report addicts, but not
required. Five hundred addicts for the entire
country are listed.
4. Addicts can purchase legal narcotics at licensed
pharmacies at very reasonable prices on prescription.
5. Sale or manufacture through other than legal
channels is prohibited.

Consequences of the British system: Very small
number of addicts, no smuggling or illegal traffic, no
"contagion," no addict-crime.

Summary and conclusions by the author.

The Shanghai Conference of 1909 was instigated by the U.S. because of these developments, coupled with the realization that our acquisition of the Phillipines had placed us in a peculiarly intimate relation with the Oriental opium traffic. The Conference launched the international efforts leading to attempts to bring about controls over trade and production of narcotic preparations, and, in the U.S., led to the passage of the Harrison Narcotic Act of 1914. This Act set up a licensing and control procedure for opiates, and particularly established the distinctions between legal and illegal trade and use of the drugs. Trade and use of the drugs were specifically limited to "legitimate medical use," and all others were prohibited. Not until 1919 were enforcement provisions established, and these were then tested in the courts. In the Webb case of 1919 the Supreme Court ruled that it was illegal for a physician to prescribe narcotics for a known addict, but implied that it would be legal in a treatment program designed to cure an addict. The 1922 Behrman case went a step beyond this and declared it illegal to prescribe narcotics even in a treatment program. Therefore, vigorous enforcement of the prohibitory laws was launched by the Bureau of Narcotics of the Department of Treasury. In 1953, the head of the Bureau claimed great success in this effort, on the grounds that in 1914, 1 in 460 in the population was an addict, but, by 1953, the figure had fallen to 1 in 1,000.

From the beginning of the drug prohibition period until just recently, the decisive philosophy has been founded on the assumption that strict enforcement and stiff punishment would serve to stamp out addiction, and, therefore, the traffic in illegal drugs. In other words, the emphasis has progressively been directed toward eliminating addiction rather than eliminating smuggling or the internal traffic. This is in contrast to the philosophy of liquor pro-

THE NEW DRUG PROHIBITION

TREASURY DEPARTMENT'S POSITION
ON LEGALIZING DRUGS

"The Treasury would be the last to suggest
that enforcement is the whole solution. The
Treasury has opposed the alternative of allowing
continued addiction by maintaining drug dosage,
and this has contributed to some public misunderstanding. The Treasury Department and its
Bureau of Narcotics do not favor the penitentiary
confinement of addicts in preference to treatment
and possible cure. We have never had such a
policy. In keeping with the viewpoint of the
American Medical Association we have consistently
urged treatment and cure. But we have joined the
very respectable body of authorities opposed to
the defeatist alternative of making narcotics legally
available to addicts."

*From Secretary of the Treasury Douglas Dillon's
remarks at the White House Conference on Narcotic
and Drug Abuse, 1962.*

hibition wherein the enforcement effort was directed
toward traffic rather than use. In response to the philosophy
underlying enforcement of the drug laws, there has been
a steady pressure to increase the severity of the penalties,
and to steadily advance the concept that the mere use of
narcotics as well as the illegal manufacture and sale was a
crime. In response to the pressure, which is often blamed
solely on the Bureau of Narcotics (but finding, nevertheless, sympathetic allies in Congress), a succession of laws
has been passed to increase the severity of punishment. In
addition to the federal legislation, the states, also, have

moved in the same direction, largely following the Uniform Code recommended during the early 1930s.

The Boggs Act of 1951 was one of the highlights in the legislative history. Prior to its passage, the federal sentence for "possession" was 1 to 10 years and averaged out to 1½ years. The new act provided mandatory minimum sentences of 2, 5 and 10 years for first, second, and third offenses, with no probation nor parole privileges. No distinctions were made, after the Marihuana Act of 1938, between possession of opiates (usually heroin) and marihuana. There did develop some concept of a distinction, however, between possession with the intent to use as opposed to possession with the intent to sell. In practice, the determination of "intent" came to be made by measuring the amount of drug found in the possession of the offender; if over a certain amount it was assumed that the intent was to sell. However, laws did not make any distinction in the penalties. During the period of liquor prohibition, jury

ON CURRENT ENFORCEMENT OF PROHIBITION

"Police corruption explains why the war against heroin has been a failure, a monumental waste of manpower and money."

Joseph Fisch, chief counsel of the New York State Commission of Investigation, 1971.

trials frequently ended in acquittal because of the prevalence of drinkers among the jurors. Until now, however, drug-using jurors have not extended this sort of leniency to drug offenders because of their rarity among the population selected for jury duty. The next generation might see a change in this regard.

State laws, even more than the federal laws, tended to become directed more and more punitively toward the drug user rather than the drug trafficker, apparently because of an assumption that primary responsibility for enforcement of the trade control provisions would be a federal one. By the 1950s Illinois, for instance, passed a law establishing a minimum 10-year sentence for first offenses and life imprisonment for second offenses. In Texas, in 1957, the death penalty was applied for convictions stemming from drug sales to minors. Although a few hospital facilities, including the two Public Health Service Hospitals at Lexington, Kentucky and Fort Worth, Texas, were provided for drug addict rehabilitation, the legislative and judicial attitude was clearly that hospitalization could not serve as a substitute for a prison sentence.

Thus, as these punitive laws progressed in severity and as they were tested out successfully in the courts, there developed the phenomenon of "status" crime. This term refers to the assumption that the mere fact of being a drug addict is, in itself, a crime. As this assumption became increasingly pervasive, its questionable constitutionality came to be examined. In *Robinson* v. *California,* the Supreme Court in 1962 ruled that states do not have the power to subject persons to criminal sanctions (in contrast to civil sanctions) for the sole reason of being addicted to drugs. Instead, for the first time, the Court suggested that the evidence was to the effect that addiction was an illness. Nevertheless, possession remained sufficient grounds for prosecuting the addict, even though the mere fact of addiction was now insufficient. Numerous cases have been cited of people being convicted—usually tourists after crossing

THE "STEPPING STONE" THEORY

"The relation of tobacco, especially in the form of cigarettes, and alcohol and opium is a very close one . . . morphine is the legitimate consequence of tobacco. Cigarettes, drink, opium is the logical and regular series."

From the Century, *1912, a prohibitionist magazine.*

"One particularly grave danger of habitual marihuana use is that there is often a clear pattern of graduation from marihuana to the stronger addictive opiates."

Henry Giordano, Director, U.S. Bureau of Narcotics and Dangerous Drugs, 1968.

the Mexican border into the U.S.—on simple proof of being in possession of a single marihuana cigarette. To a large extent, the massive police attention that has thus been directed toward the users, and to some extent, the local, small-scale pusher, has successfully diverted attention from the wholesaler and international smuggler.

Pressure to treat the drug user in a somewhat less criminal fashion has begun to mount during the past few years, and as a result of a strange trend in the course of events. As drug use has spread, especially in the use of the non-opiate drugs, the offenders have come to be found in all classes of society and in younger age groups. It has become increasingly easy for police to detect and arrest young people having marihuana, particularly, in their possession; and the very numbers thus identifiable as potential prison inmates not to mention that many of them might be members of prominent families of the community, makes the automatic punitive type of disposition seem increasingly unfeasible. Proposals to make marihuana possession a misdemeanor instead of a felony are often said to be received more hospitably if the governor's son has recently been arrested.

From the beginning of the 1920s, when prohibition became the dominant mode used in the U.S. of coping with the drug problem, it has often been stated or implied that success in stamping out addiction would result from the deterrent embodied in punitive measures. As time has gone on, and in spite of the enforcement efforts, the problem has increased instead of decreased; nevertheless, the same theory has been pursued. It was concluded, periodically, that any current lack of success stemmed from the fact that laws were not punitive enough, and the answer, therefore, was to increase their severity.

The lack of any really objective appraisal of existing laws is apparent in some of the glaring contradictions in them. For instance, heroin (acetylmorphine) is known medically to have pharmacological properties essentially identical with morphine, yet heroin is completely banned from use, medically or otherwise, whereas morphine is not. Morphine is on the control list of drugs on the strength of its being a potent addictive drug (which it is), but so is codeine, which is not in the same class at all in terms of addictive potential. On the other hand, the synthetic analgesics dilaudid and demerol are comparable to morphine in all its medical properties, as well as its potential for abuse; and yet they have not been on the controlled list. Marihuana, like heroin, is also banned from all (legal) uses, in spite of the fact that it is freely available almost anywhere, and is in no way comparable to the morphine-like drugs in its abuse potential. A common argument in favor of punitive laws is that such measures serve to make traffic in drugs unprofitable, which ignores the lesson the nation learned during the days of liquor prohibition—namely, prohibition is what makes the traffic profitable (to certain kinds of entrepreneurs). Furthermore, strict prohibition confines the traffic to the professionals who, in the U.S., have come to be inseparable from the Mafia.

During the past few years, when the incidence of marihuana use has extended into larger and larger groups in the population, each local community's law-enforcement system finds it necessary to confine arrests to some token percentage of users, and thus it becomes highly selective about which ones are arrested. It is now safe to state that mere use, or even possession, of marihuana in itself is insufficient as criteria for making an arrest (although still illegal). Something else has to be added to the picture, otherwise the courts and jails would be overflowing with young local users. Certain kinds of dress, certain types of habits or behavior, which middle-class white society looks on with disfavor might be used as the additional criteria. Minority races are more likely to be arrested than whites. A group of young people driving a car under circumstances that could be looked on as a danger or nuisance become likely subjects for arrests on grounds of possession. College students are more likely to be arrested for possession during a period of actual or threatened campus unrest than at other times. Any suspicion of radicalism can become the additional factor needed. In some jurisdictions, police have found that apprehension or the threat of arrest of teenage children from certain families can be used to extract favors or blackmail. Consequently, these trends have taken the same turn that events took during liquor prohibition days. The legalization of search without warrant is now being widely used by the police under the guise that the search is for drugs, when, in fact, the search is for something else.

This device is used, for instance, to break up suspected sexual activity at drive-in movies, and to get evidence against persons accused of radical political activity. Com-

ON PUNITIVE STRATEGIES

"First of all, the technique which was used basically to meet the post-war increase in drug addiction—this technique of deterrence by terror, the technique of increased prison sentences as the answer—'make the penalties severe enough and enforce them effectively enough and addiction will disappear'—That is a beautiful formula but, unfortunately, it is unrealizable."

Judge Morris Ploscowe, reporting on the American Bar Association-American Medical Association Report on Drug Addiction, White House Conference on Narcotic and Drug Abuse, September, 1962.

plaints by young people that the marihuana allegedly found in their possession by the police was put there by the police as a device for achieving some other objective are not uncommon.

As during prohibition days, the frequency with which marihuana users especially, and heroin users to a lesser extent, managed to get away with both purchasing and using drugs, and the (real or apparent) arbitrary nature of police arrests, tend to have a profound effect in breeding contempt for the law. In both prohibition periods, success in outwitting the law became a national pastime and sign of manliness. Stanley Yolles, director of the National Institute of Health, estimated that by 1969, at least 8 to 10 million

Americans had experimented in the use of marihuana alone. Since all of these persons are implied criminals, by definition of the laws, it indicates a degree of disrespect for the law that may well account for many of the other social problems facing our nation. In 1965, the total number of crimes known to the police throughout the country reached a total of 3,665,000—only half to one-third constituting drug law violations. In California, one-fourth of all felony complaints (not convictions) in 1968 were for drug violations, and led to 34,000 adult and 17,000 juvenile arrests. Ninety-eight percent of those arrested in California had had no previous trouble with the law. Of all persons arrested in 1968 for drug violations, 57 percent were released or acquitted. One would be tempted to conclude, from these kinds of figures, that if no drug laws existed to be violated, the nation could get by with only a fraction of the present police manpower, or, instead, free what we have to attack large-scale, organized crime.

All crime data indicate a steady rise in the arrest rate of juveniles in recent years, most of whom are first offenders. Although this trend is usually interpreted as an indication of something that is happening to youth, it has also been suggested that it might be more indicative of what is happening to the police. According to this view, the offender-prone public generally outdistances the police in education, sophistication, and resourcefulness. As a result, it is conjectured, police attention comes to be directed more and more toward those offenders with whom it is easier to cope. Consequently, the seasoned, experienced, and skillful offender gets less and less police attention whereas the inexperienced, easy-to-catch juveniles get more and more, thus producing an apparent increase in the crime rate among youthful offenders. The well-known fact that probably less than 10 percent of crimes committed ever lead to an arrest would offer plenty of maneuverability by which to make such spurious shifts in rates possible. The current trend is to concentrate a large amount of police attention on juvenile drug offenders, even though only a small percentage of these are actually singled out for arrest.

The drug prohibition laws clearly have produced effects opposite to those predicted, since the problem is worse now than it ever was. Rarely, however, has anyone responsible for the enforcement at high levels been prepared to admit failure. With increasing frequency, attacks on past programs take the form of regarding enforcement as the *cause*, rather than the *cure*, of the problem. Clearly, the serious social problems generated during liquor prohibition days were *caused* to a considerable extent by prohibition, in exchange for which it would be difficult to find any redeeming value for the laws. If this indictment of prohibition programs is regarded as excessive, even if partly true, reference might be made to the British system under

NATIONAL COMMISSION ON MARIHUANA AND DRUG ABUSE, 1971

"In the case of marihuana control legislation, legal penalties were originally assigned with total disregard for the medical and scientific evidence about the properties of the drug or its effects. Harsh penalties, and thus the law, becomes a mockery if they are based on unsubstantiated theory or folklore. I know of no clearer evidence in which the punishment for an infraction of the law is more harmful than the crime."

Jesse Steinfeld, M.D., Surgeon General, U.S. Public Health Service.

which there is almost no prohibition, and essentially no drug problem. Until recently, too many American leaders assumed that Britain had no prohibition because it had no problem, but that because we had a problem, we therefore must have prohibition. Now, this thinking is being turned around to say that, possibly, Britain has no problem because it has no prohibition, and we have a problem because we have prohibition. Using this same view, it can also be stated that, during the days of liquor prohibition, we had a major set of social and political problems associated with illicit traffic in alcohol, plus the problem of alcoholism.

LEGALIZATION OF MARIHUANA: PUBLIC OPINION

"Public opinion polls indicate that only about one-sixth of our people favor legalization; the rest disapprove. Since the prospect of immediately repealing all restrictive laws regarding the sale and use of marihuana appears to be remote, some less destructive system than the present one is desirable. Repealing overly punitive laws against simple possession of small quantities (not over two ounces, for example) is one currently popular suggestion.

Obviously, some decision regarding future action is necessary. Since the warning signals that marihuana can be harmful are numerous, widespread, and apparently increasing, it would seem to be sound social policy to discourage its use by all reasonable methods until or unless future research proves it has no deleterious effects."

From Legalization of Marijuana: Pros and Cons, *Dana Farnsworth, M.D.,* American Journal of Psychiatry, *August, 1971.*

At the present time, without liquor prohibition, we have only the problem of alcoholism. Legal means had no effect on the problem of alcoholism, either during the prohibition period or during the time of non-prohibition.

History may be repeating itself insofar as prohibition of marihuana is concerned. In this respect, marihuana shares some of the aspects of alcohol use. Furthermore, many of the more detached, perhaps more scientific, observers of the drug scene find youthful marihuana users taking to the drug instead of to alcohol *because* it is prohibited. The deliberate defiance of the establishment is, undoubtedly, a motivation that prompts many young people to elect this route, and if marihuana were not prohibited, some other token of defiance would be resorted to. The traditionalists do not see this set of circumstances as any reason for liberalizing the laws, however, for to do so, to them, would be an admission of defeat.

PROPOSALS TO LIBERALIZE DRUG LAWS

At the time the narcotic and marihuana prohibition laws were passed by Congress, unlike the situation surrounding the passage of the Eighteenth Amendment, there was essentially no opposition, no lobbying against the laws, no public sentiment advocating leniency, and apparently no vested interests seeking to maintain the status quo. As a result, the Congress generally accepted the recommendations for legislation made by the Bureau of Narcotics, held no hearings, and never questioned the arguments presented in favor of prohibition. As narcotic traffic and use continued to increase in spite of the enforcement efforts, Congress then accepted unquestioningly the Bureau's plea for increasing the severity of the laws and seemed unconcerned over the way attention was being diverted from the traffic to the user.

The plea for liberalizing the laws first originated only some 10 or so years ago from young people who were, themselves marihuana users, and, as such, their pleas had little impact. Some unobtrusive and unpublicized recommendations from certain medical circles also had arisen favoring the British system of narcotics control. These also failed to have any significant impact. However, during the past very few years, a growing number of judges, attorneys general and others who have had direct experience in the enforcement area have come out for more liberal policies. These, finally, are beginning to be noticed, and taken seriously, even by legislators. A prominent attorney, John Kaplan, published a book titled *Marijuana, The New Prohibition* in 1970 that made a scholarly and objective case for legalizing marihuana (only). Judging by the wide distribution of this book, it is likely to have considerable influence. More and more, Congressmen are prepared to admit privately today that they favor a liberalization of the laws, although they tend to continue making public statements to the contrary. The White House Conference on Narcotic and Drug Abuse (1963) was inspired by President Kennedy and his brother, the Attorney General, as a move to provide, for the first time, a forum for the more liberal sentiments then rising. A conspicuous feature of the conference was a ceremony announcing the retirement of the long-time Director of the Federal Bureau of Narcotics, Harry J. Anslinger, who was known for his authorship of most of the punitive federal laws. The ceremony symbolized to many conferees present the end of that era, although, disappointingly, the old director was succeeded by Henry Giordano who had very similar view-points.

Few public debates or investigations on the issue ever enjoy the advantage of having the pros and cons of prohibition aired in anything like an objective manner. The spokesmen for each side tend to discredit themselves in the eyes of the other by their very evident biases and short-sightedness. The real public issue should focus on, but never has, a careful weighing of all the costs of prohibition—the monetary, the manpower, and the social costs—against its benefits—and not promised benefits, but real ones. The supporters of the prohibition status quo, typically, base their arguments on the patently absurd assumption that enforcement actually works in curbing use of and traffic in drugs. Too often, the proponents of liberalization or repeal base their arguments on an appeal to permit the young to do what they choose with their lives, their morals, and their careers without interference. This plea ignores the fact that the public sees this stand as something being advocated for their own children, and will not buy it. Young people's judgment is not trusted, least of all by their parents.

Both the public and the police have a marked tendency to see the difference between drug users and non-drug users as equivalent to the difference between the "good guys" and the "bad guys." When, for instance, it is pointed out that there are gross and inequitable inconsistencies between the legalization of alcohol and the prohibition of drugs, the public views this as merely another similar difference—the majority of "good" people can be trusted to handle their liquor, but the minority of others cannot be trusted to handle their drugs.

From the growing list of proposals that have advocated

liberalizing changes in the drug laws, some examples might
be cited, graded from the most extreme to the least extreme,
as they might apply to marihuana only.

1. The most extreme position would appear to be one
that merely advocates the repeal of existing restricting
legislation, with no laws or other controls to take its place
except the pressures of public opinion and education. Before the passage of the Harrison Act in 1914, this was the
situation that prevailed in the U.S., and, although it might
be admitted that that condition was not good, it could be
claimed that it was no worse than the one prevailing now,
and it cost nothing to maintain. Assuming that, under any
conditions, drug abuse would continue to be disapproved
of socially, this move would be equivalent to the use of
profanity in polite conversation—legal but "not nice." A
similar approach is also being advocated in the repeal of
anti-abortion laws.

2. A less extreme position would be to repeal the existing laws, thus legalizing the use and sale of marihuana,
but exerting some small degree of control through taxation
and making it illegal to sell to minors. This proposal would
make the use and sale of the drug then equivalent to the
way in which tobacco is handled—another product claimed
to have harmful effects on people who use it.

3. A still less extreme position would be a modification
of the second one. It would seek to discourage, or at least
avoid encouraging, drug use by removing the profit incentive from the traffic. Ostensibly, if profits can be made,
there would be forces brought to bear to expand and increase the use of the drug. One obvious way to achieve
this could be to make the government itself the one to
market the legalized product, and to exact high enough
taxes to make its use expensive, but not so high as to encourage bootlegging. The legalized forms of gambling

(lottery) in some states would be equivalent to this method.

4. Another modified position would be to legalize sale and use, but restrict both to licensed, tightly controlled personnel. This is essentially the method used in the control of prescription drugs; and in the case of the sedative–narcotic–analgesic drugs, the parallels with marihuana are much greater than the differences. This system might provide varying degrees of conditions to qualify a person to be a user, and sales would be restricted to registered pharmacists. A qualified person would need some sort of license or prescription to entitle him to buy, but this would be subject to forfeiture if the person was found to have engaged in socially dangerous activities. The Swedish system of liquor prohibition, apparently the only one that ever worked, follows these principles.

5. Another position that would come fairly close to the present system would be to remove the restrictions and penalties on use or possession for use, but continue to attack the traffic in marihuana. This was essentially the way in which liquor prohibition was handled, and although it certainly did not work, it might prove to be worth at least a trial run.

6. Last, the least extreme position, and the one that current trends indicate is most likely to happen in the near future, is one that makes no changes in the laws themselves, but allows enforcement to gradually disappear. This is the rather universal way in which laws against prostitution, gambling, pornography, and other so-called vices are handled by society. Enforcement is merely a sporadic and token gesture designed to prevent violations that are too flagrant. As long as violations are discrete or confined to suitable portions of the community, they are tolerated.

7. Another method, which would not fit into any

particular place on the hierarchial list according to how
extreme it is, would be one that permits each state to establish its own code. This would require repeal of the federal
laws, except perhaps those concerning smuggling and
illegal manufacture. Conceivably, various states would
adopt laws and systems of enforcement of varying degrees
of liberality. This would permit, then, a citizen to make his
home in the state in which the laws suit his tastes. This system already is well established in respect to laws legalizing
gambling and divorce.

LIBERALIZING NARCOTIC LAWS

Until recently, "hard" narcotic use had tended
to be limited to ghetto residents of the very large metropolitan centers of the country. Although never yielding to enforcement efforts, the extent of use tended to remain rather
narrowly confined. Because of the population affected and
the fact that there seemed to be no great contagion of use,
little interest was shown in liberalizing the laws on use or
possession (usually, of heroin). In only the past few years,
however, the practice has appeared to have spread widely.
How real the spread is in terms of numbers of new users is
uncertain, but the news media tend to create the impression
that, for the first time, all classes of society and all parts
of the country are now vulnerable. Again, as with marihuana, the prospects of middle-class, suburban-dwelling
young people and college students being sentenced to long
prison terms for possession of heroin has triggered a growing interest in more lenient approaches. Clearly, however,
the majority of public sentiment and most public pronouncements continue to take the hard line. The recent
news of American military men in Viet Nam being in-

creasingly exposed to heroin use has also lent a new non-punitive slant to the more objective deliberations on the subject. Indicative of the very recent turn in attitude is the army's decision to reverse the practice of giving disciplinary discharges to drug users from combat zones.

The prototype most often referred to, which contrasts vividly with the American system of drug prohibition, is the British system. In Britain, very little legislation has been brought to bear on drugs and the British authorities claim they have, essentially, no problem. There is no illegal smuggling or traffic in hard drugs and no evidence of drug-related crime. Instead, drug addicts are permittted to register with the National Health Service to receive regular prescriptions for drugs, which they then purchase at drugstores at very reasonable prices. The physicians who do the prescribing are requested to make every effort to cure the addicts, and to instigate a program of progressive diminution in the dosage. Only 500 or so addicts have been registered.

When the British model is cited as a more desirable one to follow than our own, the advocates of our punitive system claim that the British need no prohibition because they have no drug problem. Opponents of our system, on the other hand, reason the other way—namely, that the British have no problem *because* they have no prohibition. This argument is typical of the general tendency to over-simplify the cause-and-effect relationships among drug use and other factors. Another example is the crusade of the Bureau of Narcotics to prove that drug use causes crime, on the grounds that the two are often linked together; the linkage, however, is most often caused by the fact that known drug users have police records for possession of drugs. A more objective view would emphasize that the same kind of people who get into trouble with the law are likely to be those who also use drugs, drink alcohol to excess, gamble, and engage in many other anti-social activities. To say that any one of these practices is the cause of the other is dreadfully short-sighted.

The chance of the United States adopting the British system in the near future seems very remote, regardless of how logical such a move might be. However, a compromise is available that seems more acceptable. A new morphine-like drug (methadone), having essentially the same properties, has been used in experimental clinics to wean heroin addicts off their drugs. Actually, the program merely substitutes one drug for another, but the new one has the advantages of being legal, costing less, being of dependable quality, and allowing the user to function in society (i.e., to maintain a job, etc.). Inasmuch as this substitution has been given the label of "treatment," and has acquired rather high status, it is quite conceivable that the legalization on a wide scale of methadone substitution for heroin, under a physician's guidance, could be instituted and achieve essentially the same effects as would adoption of the British system. One deterrent would be that drug addicts themselves might be misled into not trying the method because they, too, might subscribe to the euphemism that it constitutes "treatment." Already, however, a blackmarket has developed in this new drug, and in the blackmarket it is used interchangeably with heroin. This trend would seem to indicate that the drug addicts, are, perhaps, more sophisticated than the non-drug-using public.

LEGALIZING ONE DRUG, NOT OTHERS

There have been several instances in recent years illustrating what happened to the patterns of drug use when a particular drug became either more or less available. Most often these instances have involved wide fluctuations in marihuana availability. The impression gained by many who have studied the subject is that the number of users tends to remain constant, but that preferences shift to the drug that is most available at any given time. California police noticed an increase in heroin use on one occasion when extensive inroads were made on the marihuana supply. This situation is somewhat similar to what happened to American drinking patterns during prohibition, when the availability of a particular kind of alcoholic preparation determined the preferences.

If the drug laws are liberalized, it seems most likely that the first attempts will be directed only toward marihuana, not opiates nor the exotic drugs. If past experience is indicative of drug users' general behavior, then a shift toward the use of marihuana and away from the other drugs, and perhaps even away from alcohol, can be expected. This shift would present what might then look like an increase in the amount of marihuana use, and this could create alarm. However, the evidence at hand seems to indicate that, of all the substances with which people might intoxicate themselves, marihuana appears to be the least serious. It is less addicting, less toxic, and less likely to be associated with dangerous activities, probably even less so than alcohol. In other words, an increase in marihuana use would not be as bad as it might appear to be.

Chapter
9

SOLUTIONS: MANAGING THE DRINKING PROBLEM IN INDUSTRY

DRINKING PROBLEMS IN INDUSTRY

Numerous surveys from various sources, as well as reports from industrial physicians, indicate that one of the major costs of problem drinking in industry is its relationship to absenteeism. Although only after careful and expert investigations are conducted does the truth become apparent, it is evident that drinking is far and away the commonest cause of absenteeism, with the common cold and family problems following it in frequency. A not inconsiderable cost, but one that is impossible to measure, is the relationship between organizational morale and problem drinking. Morale is likely to be adversely affected when key people in the organization set an undesirable drinking example, or when it becomes evident to employees that certain personnel are managing to get away with violations of organizational rules with their drinking, and when the drinking man defaults on his responsibilities and throws the burden of his work on his fellow employees. Few problem drinkers earn the sympathy of their fellow workers when the drinking interferes with their work. The one single situation over which management has control and that can be manipulated by management to reduce the magnitude of the problem is the example-setting behavior of key executives, who, instead, are more likely in many organizations to be regarded as immune to the rules that apply to hourly workers.

Other costs attributable to problem drinking include accidents to other employees and equipment, serious errors in business judgment, and an increased turnover rate among the drinkers, who are inclined to be less dependable than other employees.

However, the drinking man exhibits characteristics and habits that serve, also, to conceal the nature and scope of his problem so that the typical organization becomes aware of only the most obvious cases. It might be reasonable to estimate that even the most careful study and estimate of the scope of problem drinking in any large organization would succeed in identifying only one-half to two-thirds of the total involved. The unidentified group would be made up of those individuals who were either more skillful than others in concealing their problem, or of those whose problem had not yet invaded the work situation.

Only recently has there been widespread concern about the problem of the drug user in industry. Although less attention-getting because of its greater degree of familiarity, the alcohol-related problem is far more serious than the problem of drug abuse. In any event, industrial organizations can approach the drug problem in essentially the same way that they approach the alcohol problem, so we need not give it separate consideration here. One relatively large potential problem area that will generally go undetected and unrecognized involves people who regularly take prescription drugs under a doctor's care. The mere fact of being "legal" and "respectable" as a result of being under a doctor's care, however, does not change any of the facts concerning drug effects. Whatever policy is adopted should apply equally to these cases. The point is that both legal and illegal drugs that affect the central nervous system have the same effects on human judgment and performance as does alcohol. Thus, if it is dangerous for a truck driver to work while under the influence of alcohol, it is equally dangerous if he is under the influence of illegal marihuana or "respectable," physician-prescribed tranquilizers or mood-elevators.

Organizations rarely have developed a rational and consistent policy on how to cope with alcohol problems, in spite of the fact that most large companies that have been in operation over substantial periods of time have come to be well aware of the problem. Unions and management rarely collaborate to establish a uniform policy, even though solutions to the problem are in the interest of both.

Essentially, no nation-wide program has ever had any significant effect on the alcohol problem, usually because each has relied on ineffective moralistic or punitive platitudes that serve only to gratify the interests of people who are not themselves problem drinkers and who have little or no effect on those people the programs are meant to reach. In other words, traditional educational programs or organizational practices tend mostly to make the abstainers feel good about their abstinence.

An approach that has never been used extensively is one that deserves widespread experimentation. This approach to the problem would be the adoption of industry-wide, uniform, consistently enforced, policies that employ the leverage afforded by the worker's reliance on his job, his esteem for his job, and the fact that a major share of his time is spent on the job. No other factor, except the influence of family, can have the impact that this leverage could exercise. However, the influence must be carefully designed to bring about an effect that is equally advantageous to both the organization and the employee himself (otherwise they would not cooperate). To be of mutual benefit, a policy had better not resemble other traditional programs that have been based primarily on punitive or moralistic threats.

The prospects of instantly inaugurating an industry-wide policy would, of course, be fraught with nearly insurmountable obstacles. However, profit-making organizations (at least) do respond favorably at times to progress made by other individual organizations that give them a competitive advantage. Therefore, if a few organizations successfully adopted a policy that yielded desirable results, this precedent would more than likely be followed by many others, and the prospects for an industry-wide policy could become a reality. The competitive advantage obtained by an organization that adopts a sound policy could be manifested in both increased advantages in recruiting desirable employees and in reducing labor costs. Federal civil service is also in a particularly strategic position for setting examples for industry to follow, as it has already done in inaugurating fringe-benefits.

Most efforts to describe the on-the-job alcohol problem tend to base their arguments on estimates of the numbers of people involved and the costs that result. The numbers involved are high, but, unfortunately, have no reliable base on which to make them sound credible. The numbers cited (for instance, the one that states that 10 percent of the working population is made up of problem drinkers) might, in fact, be accurate, but there is little solid evidence to either prove or disprove them. It should be enough to state,

and perhaps much more believable, that the alcohol problem is big and costly. Furthermore, it is safe to say that no
organization (and this includes church organizations) can
regard itself as free of the problem.

Certain trades, occupations, and enterprises tend to attract more than the average share of problem drinkers.
Those that employ people with less sophisticated skills,
those that afford relatively little supervision of employees
(house painters, salesmen), and those that tend to employ
people who are transient and have only loose family ties
(merchant marine, traveling construction crews) are most
likely to attract the problem drinker. It need not be mentioned that those jobs that offer the prospect of easy access
to free drinks, such as bartending, are especially likely to
attract large numbers of problem drinkers. Less well recognized, however, is the kind of job sought by the drinker
who is generally more careful both in concealing his drinking habits and in finding secure kinds of employment. Thus,
civil service jobs attract a substantial number, and because
college professorships afford a high degree of security,
these positions will attract many applicants from the drinking population. A major source of danger to the national
economy and security arises from the fact that many positions of high influence in public life also offer the security
sought by problem drinkers. There is an unsubstantiated,
and perhaps apocryphal, rumor, for instance, that the
United States Senate has its own AA unit, or, if not, that it
should have.

It is not uncommon for organizations, particularly their
personnel departments, to minimize the extent of their
alcohol problem because of a common human tendency.
Problem drinkers are likely to acquire considerable skill
in concealing their drinking, and, if they are exposed, those
persons responsible for hiring or supervising them are

rarely willing to admit that they have been taken in. In the process of arriving at reliable estimates of the extent of drinking problems in a given organization, it would be realistic to assume that the correct number can be found only by multiplying those counted by some constant. The true number is likely to be double the estimated number.

In spite of his efforts to conceal his drinking, the drinker will also exhibit other characteristics that can be detected and recognized as part of the same set of problems. The other manifestations might include either those that are directly related to the drinking itself (e.g. the kind of excuses given for missing work), or those that characterize the kind of person who is most likely to be a problem drinker. These manifestations might be referred to as "symptomatic," if related directly to drinking, and "characterological," if derived from personality characteristics. However, not all heavy drinkers allow their drinking habits to interfere with their work. It is quite conceivable that, with proper and careful placement, dependable work can be performed by some people who, outside of work, drink excessively. Improper placement, however, might well impose the problem on the job. Sooner or later, in other words, the problem drinker is very likely to become known as a problem to the organization, but not necessarily through the drinking itself. Nevertheless, it is possible and feasible for a sound personnel policy to minimize or even eliminate these problems in many instances. A policy based on eliminating all drinkers from the personnel ranks is doomed to failure for they are too numerous and too difficult to detect to make such a simple policy feasible. What is feasible, however, is a policy that protects the job situation from the problems of drinking. A successful policy in this respect, also serves the person who is potentially a problem. Much time and effort in establishing a policy will inevitably be directed toward detecting the problem drinker. Without a more extensive policy that deals fairly and responsibly with the problem, once detected, this limited goal would have little value.

A PHILOSOPHIC BASE FOR A POLICY ON PROBLEM DRINKING

More traditional approaches to the issue of problem drinking were apt to adopt a philosophy that cast the problem in either moralistic or medical terms. That is, the problem drinker was regarded either as some sort of evil person, or as "sick." Unfortunately, many otherwise progressive managements have followed this second aspect of the theory in the misguided notion that it was more enlightened than considering a drinker evil. In neither case, however, does the theory offer a logical approach to a sound personnel policy in coping with the problem, once it is detected. A practical theory or philosophy is one that offers clues to solutions to problems, even if at the expense of playing down the importance of delineating causes. Instead of the moral versus medical choice usually considered, it would be more fruitful to regard the problem drinker as being primarily a person who copes with responsibility in an immature way. With this view in mind, significant personnel policy implications become self-evident. For instance, it would follow, and it would be correct to conclude, that a problem drinker would not likely respond to cool and rational logic, that he would not likely do his best without supervision, and that it would not be wise to commit major responsibilities of the organization to his care. Nevertheless, it would also follow that under conditions of reduced responsibility—particularly as shown by reduced demands for decisions on his part—he might perform at his best—

whatever his best might be. Also, like children, he would more likely respond to rewards than to punishment, and giving him attention could be more important in sustaining his interest in his job than it might be for other personnel. Furthermore, as is the case with children, ignoring unsatisfactory behavior often yields better results than punishing it.

Another philosophic concept that would be appropriate for an employer to adopt would be to regard the drinking problem as his business only when it intrudes on the work situation, meaning that it would not be the organization's responsibility to influence what happens to the drinker outside of work. It is further fitting and appropriate that the employer exercise a very considerable leverage in exercising influence through the power he has to offer: to withdraw or to deny a man a job, as well as to reward or fail to reward good performance through salary raises, promotions, and other emoluments. Having this power and influence also implies a considerable responsibility, since it could be used to either make or break a man. In most cases, fortunately, what is good for the organization will also be good for the employee, so that there is no inherent and inevitable conflict. That is to say, any policy that effectively seeks to ensure good employee performance will benefit both parties concerned, assuming that the employee, as well as the organization, is properly rewarded when successful.

DETECTING THE PROBLEM DRINKER AND DRUG USER

Several clues are indicative of the existence of a problem, and when one is alerted to their significance, they can be effectively used to detect the problem. It is safe

to state, however, that no single clue cited will be sufficiently diagnostic to be convincing in itself. In other words,
more than one is needed, and the more found, the greater
the degree of confidence one can have in the conclusion.
Some of the clues are:

1. When the opportunity is made available to witness
the behavior of groups of personnel in a social situation
where drinking is normally taking place, the problem drinkers are likely to stand out from the rest in the way in which
they conduct themselves. The detection, however, not only
involves identifying those who drink much more than the
rest of the group, or who seem to get drunker than the rest.
Although this is one clue, it is so obvious that even the
problem drinker realizes it, and may find ways to conceal it.
He might, for instance, do all or most of his drinking before
the party, so that the amount he drinks is not unusual. He
might abstain altogether, which is another possible clue,
for he might well realize how dangerous it is for him to
drink in public (dangerous to his reputation, that is). His
drinking might be more surreptitious than is the case with
other people, or more rapid, or more likely to include
strong (high alcohol content) drinks. Also, his behavior
is likely to be different, but not solely in terms of how
inebriated he appears. Long-standing drinkers often learn
to conduct themselves with unusual decorum, even with a
heavy load of alcohol in them. Above all, if they behave in
ways that seem distinctly different from their sober ways,
this becomes a very convincing clue. The quiet person
might become noisy, the peaceful one belligerent, the
gloomy one hilarious, and so on.

2. Long-standing acquaintance with the problem drinker
reveals an unusual skill not often apparent in other people.
He is very apt to be not only greatly preoccupied with, but
also highly informed about, the details of liquor logistics.

He knows the clerks personally, the locations, the closing times, and the prices of various liquor stores, and which ones will cash his checks. He will spend a carefully allocated portion of his time, with few oversights, in seeing to it that his liquor supply is replenished. Similarly, the drug user spends an inordinate amount of his time replenishing his supply. People who share rides to work with the drinking man are especially likely to witness this kind of preoccupation. Furthermore, the problem drinker will place a high priority on allocating his personal resources (financial, etc.) to the maintenance of his liquor supply; thus, perhaps, accumulating debts in other cost areas.

3. The problem of absenteeism can be more pervasive than merely taking off days for either binges or hangovers. The problem drinker will find more than the usual number of excuses for absenting himself from actual work, including maximizing vacation time, sick leave, lunch hours, coffee breaks, or unduly prolonging tangential duties that take him away from actual work. It is aptly stated that "work is the curse of the drinking class." Nevertheless, the careful drinker can manage to conceal a great deal of wasted time under an umbrella of apparent diligence. The clever ones will find ways of circumventing systems of time accountability. Explanations for absences, often convincingly supported by excuses from wives, are often learned from long practice, and thus likely to be disarming to others. Too often, personnel departments or managers are misled by the reasons given for absences rather than the number of absences, and the important issue of work performance in relation to organizational requirements needs to be viewed only in terms of the number, not the reasons.

4. An unusual number of problem drinkers, after substantial experience with drinking, turn up with some sort of stomach trouble, and complaints of this sort, or medical

attention for them, is often an important clue to an underlying drinking problem.

5. Another characteristic phenomenon is the tendency
for problem drinkers to become involved in more accidents
than other people do. Perhaps most significantly, they tend
to get involved in bizarre accidents. Thorough investigation
of these unusual occurrences often shows that the accident
in question was not really so bizarre as it originally seemed,
because the person involved was "under the influence." A
common example is smoking in bed, falling asleep, and
setting the bed on fire (only likely to happen to someone
whose level of consciousness has been substantially attenuated). Auto accidents are extraordinarily common, and the
more careful problem drinkers have already recognized this
danger and avoid driving (in itself an unusual habit in
modern society).

6. The male problem drinker has often managed to
establish an unusual relationship with a woman—mother,
wife, landlady, girl friend. These relationships are unusual
in that there appears to be an absence of any kind of
positive affection, yet a great deal of dependency. These
women serve to protect the drinker from the scrapes he gets
into and they contribute both to his survival and to a con-
tinuation of his drinking patterns. Family life is equally
unusual, being characterized either by total disruption or
by frequent crises. Another sign of the problem drinker is
to find a middle-aged man, still unmarried, living with his
mother. Multiple marriages are frequent among the group,
and successive wives or husbands tend to be remarkably
alike.

7. Among older problem drinkers, when past records are
surveyed for purposes of hiring or promotion, it is common
to find significant gaps in their histories that cannot be

adequately accounted for. These periods might have been associated with long periods of heavy drinking and no job, or times when they had been discharged for drinking, or other telltale incidents that they hesitate to reveal. Their work performance history is not likely to be consistent nor show steady achievement; the pattern will be erratic and reveal a history of unfinished starts, such as failure to finish college.

8. Female problem drinkers are not so likely as men to seek jobs in industry. Instead, they are more apt to be found working, or seeking employment, in more protected, less competitive fields, such as in restaurants and hospitals. The real or apparent rarity of the female problem drinker in industry is probably responsible for the scarcity of studies concerning them.

9. Long-standing problem drinkers who have managed to hold on to jobs fairly well will usually have developed considerable skill in concealing their problem, and this skill is apt to spill over into other areas. As a result, they are inclined to present rather convincing impressions of their capabilities. This skill is almost a necessary concomitant to having attained a certain degree of job success. Furthermore, this skill itself is not infrequently exploited by employers when they use these people for selling or public relations work.

10. Fellow workers are in a position to detect other characteristics of the problem drinker that are associated with his peer relationships. He is very likely to keep himself apart from others in many ways, or to go to the other extreme and become a kind of leader in extracurricular (non-work) activities. Above all, he tends to exhibit a kind of insensitivity to the public opinion that governs much of the behavior of others.

RECRUITING, PLACING, AND
RETAINING PROBLEM DRINKERS

As mentioned before, it is impossible to simply try to avoid employing all problem drinkers because there are too many of them in any population and they are too difficult to identify. Drug users, on the other hand, are far less frequent and an avoidance policy directed toward them conceivably would be more feasible. They might, however, show a sharp increase among young recruits. Nevertheless, careful management and placement of the problem drinker could yield desirable results.

The central issue to consider in hiring, placing, and retaining an employee who is strongly suspected of having a serious alcohol problem is responsibility. A measure of the amount of responsibility required of a job can be determined by estimating the degree of risk entailed, to him or the organization, in the decisions he is asked to make. Typically, the problem drinker will cope well with less responsibility than his technical ability would indicate. He might be an expert auto mechanic, for instance, but quite unreliable in estimating the cost of a job. Too often in industry the only available route for advancement is through assuming increasing levels of responsibility. Reward systems for superior technical performance that are not based solely on management career ladders need to be provided in nearly every organization. Too often, a promotion entails losing a good mechanic and gaining a poor supervisor. Although this dilemma applies in many ways to the management of an efficient organization, it is especially critical in placing a person with a drinking problem.

Saying that a place might be found in an organization for a problem drinker should not be construed to mean that some should not be excluded. Which ones are to be screened out of the system and which ones are to be screened in, or kept in, is an important part of a sound organizational policy. A well-advertised policy that is consistently followed could become a very important factor in reducing the problem of alcohol in industry. An example of a rather simple, easily understood policy would be one that makes any conflict between drinking and job performance cause for dismissal or demotion, except that each case would be considered eligible for one, but only one, second chance.

Supervising the problem drinker is the critical element in retaining him. On one hand, he is likely to do his best when most of what he does is subject to supervision, but, on the other hand, excessive demands on him tend to bring out the worst in him. The secret, then, is supervision without excessive demands. Furthermore, it would make sense to relate his rewards (wages, and so on) clearly and precisely to how much work he turns out, not to how much time he puts in.

Not infrequently, the problem drinker shows convincing evidence that he has essentially solved his problem. In such cases, allocating responsibility is still a critical factor, for too much could easily provoke a recurrence of the problem. In other words, a worker who is currently coping satisfactorily with an old alcohol problem and is also handling a given amount of responsibility might well be successful only as long as the demands on him do not increase.

A few specific recommendations on job placement for the problem drinker include: (a) Avoid placing him in jobs that require him to operate almost entirely on his own, such as traveling salesman; (b) Never structure a situation such that the other people in the organization depend entirely on his performing his job at a specified time; (c) Do not require him to be constantly facing the public (customers, etc.); (d) Although supervision is necessary, do not constantly subject him to surveillance; (e) Reduce to a minimum the degree of competition with other workers; (f) Do not place him in positions requiring instantaneous and important decisions. Although these rules might seem very restrictive, they would still afford many satisfactory placements for the typical mechanic, machinist, electrician, or bookkeeper.

INGREDIENTS OF AN ORGANIZATION (OR INDUSTRY-WIDE) POLICY

Without presuming to state what a policy on problem drinkers and drug users might be, the ingredients that make up a sound policy can be specified with a minimum of controversy. These would include:

1. An effective policy will be, above all, one which is easily and widely understood by all concerned and is consistently followed. This means that any provision in a stated policy that is unduly ambiguous, or not likely to lead to dedicated and honest implementation, would not be feasible.

2. One part of the policy will state who in the organization has authority to implement it, and the possibilities include: first-line supervisors, the medical department, the personnel department, or a joint management-union committee. A policy that depends for its success on any authoritative structure other than the judgment of individuals would have to be rather narrow and rigid in scope.

3. Another part of the policy will state what rule will apply to the issue of drinking, or being under the influence of alcohol or drugs, while on the job. Any policy that pro-

hibits any imbibing during working hours must also clearly include executive personnel in its provisions.

4. In addition, the policy will state what action will be taken concerning any employee (including executives) who violates, is known to have violated, or who has been suspected of having violated the drinking-on-the-job rule.

5. Furthermore, a clear statement needs to be made about what differences in policy apply to first offenses versus subsequent offenses.

6. Also, the policy will state what the position of the organization will be on hiring a new recruit known to be, or suspected of being, a problem drinker (or drug user).

7. Last, the policy will state what responsibilities the organization accepts in the matter of rehabilitating the problem drinker, in supporting community services, and in cooperating with labor unions in shaping and implementing the policy.

THE ORGANIZATION'S ROLE IN REHABILITATION

It is essential that each organization view the problem of alcohol and drug abuse not only as a potential problem of its own, but always as a major problem of the community in which the organization has a substantial vested interest. One of the principal assets not utilized in community programs is the potential leverage inherent in the control the employer has over a person's job. Collaboration between employers and community programs might well bring about the progress that nearly all communities hope for, but have so far failed to achieve. Some of the factors that might be taken into account in designing the organization's role in community rehabilitation programs would include the following:

1. The effectiveness of any organization in adopting and following an effective alcohol-problem program will depend to a large degree on the extent of cooperation obtained from other organizations. Unions represent one of the major other organizations with a vested interest in the problem, and the other businesses of the community that adopt and follow similar policies will benefit from the united policy that results. The impetus for community-wide programs might properly originate in professional organizations or civic groups.

2. Whatever contribution a given organization makes (money, moral support, referrals, and so on) to community rehabilitation programs might properly be looked on as part of its community relations program, and the same might be said of its own internal program. Each business organization that supports rehabilitation programs in the community will serve to guarantee the program's survival (and, typically, survival rates have been poor).

3. In nearly every case of a successfully rehabilitated problem drinker, there has been some employer who gave him "another chance." Therefore, any given new change in job might well be the desirable turning point in the man's restoration to usefulness. The risk involved in making these choices might also be looked on as part of the organization's contribution to the community.

4. Large organizations might properly go so far as to introduce their own AA chapters for their employees. Access to this resource should facilitate both referral and cooperation. Keeping the problem "in the family" can prove advantageous to all concerned.

5. No action would have more impact on obtaining workers' cooperation with an alcohol-problem policy than

the courageous disciplining of an executive who has exceeded the bounds established by the policy. Few organizations appreciate the important model-setting role of executive behavior, and few appreciate the degree to which executive behavior is scrutinized by employees.

6. It is not inconceivable that the entire alcohol-problem policy might be implemented by unions rather than by management. The sense of responsibility this implies would achieve measurable benefits in upgrading the image of the union.

7. The large organization which has its own medical department might well turn over the problem to this department. When this is done, a greater than usual degree of respect for the confidentiality of employees' personal information must be respected. Once the medical department earns a reputation for holding personal information confidential, it will find itself having access to a great deal more than it would otherwise.

8. In many instances, neighboring organizations might find collaborative means of establishing joint programs, especially those pertaining to rehabilitation.

Chapter
10

SOLUTIONS: MANAGING THE NATIONAL DRUG PROBLEM

AN AMERICAN PARADOX

Historians and political scholars have often pointed out a phenomenon of American history that is seldom regarded as the fundamental contradiction it is. This paradox is the great proclivity of Americans, at all levels, to both preach and defend the principles of democratic government and democratic living while frequently resorting to restrictive laws seemingly designed to coerce people into conforming to a standardized morality. Thus, the United States has always led the way in restrictive laws attacking the personal practices of individuals. The drug and alcohol prohibitions are merely examples in a long list of similar efforts, and all have been striking failures in achieving their stated aims. Some of the other prohibitions that have been or are currently in effect include laws that seek to stamp out pornography, gambling, prostitution, unconventional sexual practices, birth control, abortions, and other practices. In no case has there ever been demonstrated an even remotely effective way to enforce any of these prohibitions. Instead, violations of the laws are universal; organized crime tends to be supported by them; police and politicians become corrupted by them; and their widely known violations encourage a profound disrespect for all laws and police in many circles. The continued demand on the part of the American public for these laws becomes a convenient way by which aspiring politicians obtain votes, but once the laws are passed both the public and the politicians become indifferent about enforcing them. It would appear that those who advocate these prohibitions are not so much interested in stamping out these practices as they are in having them officially labeled as unaccept-

DRUG ADDICTS' RESPONSE TO TREATMENT

The report summarizes efforts to engage a total of 206 heroin addicts in a drug clinic program at Massachusetts General Hospital during an 18-month period. Most were seeking methadone substitution for heroin, and in the processing of the requests, other treatment alternatives were offered. Only two patients returned for the second appointments offered them. The report concludes that the effort to engage this population in meaningful treatment was a failure. Although the offer of methadone serves to attract addicts, it did not seem to pave the way to effective withdrawal of all drugs.

Failure of Outpatient Treatment of Drug Abuse, *John O'Malley, M.D., William Anderson, M.D., and Aaron Lazare, M.D.,* American Journal of Psychiatry, *January, 1972. Author's summary.*

able behaviors. Clearly, as was the case with national prohibition in the twenties, the advocates win their case when
the law is passed, not when it is enforced. In the case of
other laws that have been the subjects of ardent crusades,
such as the civil rights laws, child labor laws, the unfair
labor practice laws, and the anti-monopoly laws, it has been
the enforcement rather than the legislation itself that became the object of interest.

It does not appear that other advanced countries are as
prone to use this legislative method of expressing moral
indignation. The British, for instance, who have a legal
system closest in character to ours, are very loath to place
legal restrictions on moral behavior, as a result of which
they have accumulated a very small number of legal prohibitions. They have recently repealed the laws prohibiting
homosexual practices among "consenting adults," and those
against having relations with mentally retarded citizens.
In more distant times in Europe, there existed a dual legal
system wherein both the state and the church had their
own laws, their own courts, and their own punishments,
with the church handling the moral issues. Perhaps in the
United States the absence of a state church that has political
power has had a lot to do with the tendency of Americans
to look to civil and criminal laws to compensate for this
lack of church power. Nevertheless, it has been largely
church-sponsored groups and crusades that have been
responsible for our restrictive laws; hence, divorce laws and
anti-birth-control laws are most restrictive in states with
the heaviest Catholic populations, whereas the anti-drug
and anti-alcohol laws have been most restrictive in the more
fundamentalist, Protestant areas.

Another way of describing this paradox is to point out
the tendency of Americans to insist on a minimum of institutionalized regulations to control their lives, on one hand,

EXTENT OF MARIHUANA USE: 1972

"On the basis of the Commission-sponsored National Survey, we have concluded that the contemporary marihuana use is pervasive, involving all segments of the U.S. population. The Survey estimated that about 24 million Americans over the age of 11 years have used marihuana at least once. . . . Until recently twice as many males as females had used it. . . . Marihuana use does not appear to vary significantly by race. . . . Usage is highest in cities, towns and suburbs, but not uncommon in rural areas. States in the Northeast and West have considerably higher rates of use than have the North Central . . . and Southern states. Use is found in all socioeconomic groups and occupations . . . those who have used the drug are heavily concentrated in the 16–25 age bracket."

Marihuana: A Signal of Misunderstanding, *First Report of the National Commission on Marihuana and Drug Abuse, March, 1972, U.S. Government Printing Office.*

and, on the other hand, to resort to laws to regulate activities that are essentially impossible to regulate, such as adultery, homosexuality, birth control, and gambling. The paradox can be explained if it is assumed that these laws are demanded for the official labels they thereby make possible rather than for the actual regulation of behavior that they apparently are intended to deal with. In other words, the laws serve to separate the "good guys" from the "bad guys" for status purposes rather than for regulatory purposes.

There might be considerable justification in using restrictive laws passed by legislatures to make "do-gooders" feel good as long as the unfeasible task of enforcing them is ignored. However, the social cost of these prohibitions has never been adequately examined, and these costs have not been weighed in the balance against their flimsy benefits. The subsidy they give to organized crime might be enough of a social cost to consider in order to justify their abolition. Another less measurable but perhaps more significant social cost is their contribution to the current disillusionment toward the American system, the current rebellion against law and order. Surely, the fall-outs from these prohibitions should prompt even the do-gooders to reconsider their support of unworkable restrictions.

REQUIREMENTS FOR SOLUTIONS

The current drug and alcohol problems are not going to improve until many people face the fact that workable systems might be, perhaps must be, those that they also find distasteful. To give a somewhat remote example, at the present time laws prohibiting prostitution are virtually universal. Nevertheless, prostitution is equally universal. Local jurisdictions that have embarked on all-out campaigns to stamp out prostitution have had the effect of merely moving the centers of activity, but in no case have they diminished the scope. In addition to all the real, non-moralistic evils that result from this illicit prostitution, it is also responsible for a growing increase in venereal disease rates. Most of the evils, except the moral ones, could be eliminated if prostitution were legalized and then controlled with adequate public health standards and other safeguards —which are probably feasible. Legalization, in other words, could effectively lead to a considerable reduction in the

ON DRUG ABUSE RESEARCH

"In response to the assertion that 'research will give us the answers about the dangers of marihuana'. . . . The danger that all are concerned about is its long-term effect. (Short-term effects are well-known.) Investigators will have to observe subjects for two to three decades before that question can be answered. Those calling for research to determine our position about marihuana have unrealistic expectations about the rapidity of a reliable response."

Sidney Cohen, Director of the Division of Narcotic Addiction and Drug Abuse of the National Institute of Health, 1969.

worst evils (organized crime, white slave trade, venereal disease, etc.). This, in other words, could be a workable solution to a current problem. However, it would be a thoroughly distasteful one to nearly every respectable person in the community. The citizens of almost every community would prefer to tolerate all the rampant evils that now stem from prostitution rather than grant it a kind of official stamp of approval. A test of true public sentiment on this score could probably be made by polling communities on their willingness to have some other (not their own) community legalize the business. Chances are that many citizens would vote in favor of other communities doing it—but it is now inconceivable that they would vote favorably if their own communities were involved.

In the old tradition that "good medicine has to taste bad," it is more than likely that the most workable solutions to the alcohol and drug problems, as with all the so-called

PERCENTAGE OF STUDENTS USING MARIHUANA WHO ALSO USE OTHER DRUGS AND STIMULANTS

OTHER DRUGS	PERCENTAGE
Alcohol	99%
Tobacco	94
Amphetamines	50
Sedatives	33
Tranquilizers	29
Hallucinogens	24

PERCENTAGE OF OPIATE USERS ALSO USING OTHER DRUGS AND STIMULANTS

OTHER DRUGS	PERCENTAGE
Alcohol	100%
Tobacco	95
Marihuana	78
Sedatives	73
Amphetamines	66
Tranquilizers	62
Hallucinogens	50

From R. H. Blum, Students and Drugs *(San Francisco: Jossey-Bass, 1969).*

"vice" problems, will be those that are also most distasteful. For instance, in many cases (e.g., legalization of marihuana), the most workable solutions might be those under which the government itself goes into the business (cf. state liquor stores), although this resort would probably prove most distasteful of all, most distasteful because it most vividly counteracts the present labeling system by placing an official stamp of approval on something that many think should be labeled "bad." Citizen resistance to permitting inmates of state prisons to work at gainful occupations represents the same order, running counter as it does to announced efforts to "rehabilitate" prisoners.

To overcome the anticipated obstacles to obtaining public support for workable solutions to the drug and alcohol problems, it might be well to speculate on other than legislative means of serving the public demands for a labeling method for disapproved behaviors. In the days of the state church, excommunication served such a purpose. An elitist society can use standards of acceptance and rejection for such purposes. An egalitarian society without an official religion is bereft of such means. Novel ways might well be construed, however. An example might be to classify certain commonly accepted social practices as privileges rather than universal rights, which a person would be disqualified

MARIHUANA ARRESTS: STATE AND FEDERAL

	STATE ARRESTS	FEDERAL ARRESTS
1965	18,815	523
1966	31,119	746
1967	61,843	941
1968	98,870	1,433
1969	118,903	2,189
1970	188,682	2,082
1971	?	3,323

(*In 1971, 60 percent of arrests led to convictions, 28.5 percent received prison sentences, and the average sentence was 39.9 months—federal cases only.*)

From Marihuana: A Signal of Misunderstanding, *Report of the National Commission on Marihuana and Drug Abuse, 1972.*

from enjoying if he were found to be an abuser of them
(not merely a normal user). Such designated privileges
might include obtaining a driver's license or credit cards.
There would be a fundamental logic in this procedure in
that the use of a driver's license or credit card entails a degree of responsibility and maturity that is wanting in someone who abuses drugs or alcohol. Thus, a new means
would arise for distinguishing the "good" from the "bad
guys," one that is related to maturity and responsibility—
in a sense, an elitist device, but nonetheless democratic to
the extent that the lines drawn would not be according to
politics, race, religion, sex, or wealth.

ANTI-PLEASURE PRINCIPLES

Cursory examination of America's vice laws,
especially by someone from another culture, tends to reach
the conclusion that they are an outgrowth of our original
Puritanism. This conclusion is somewhat doubtful when it
is considered that legislated prohibitions have increased
over time, whereas Puritanism has subsided—they have
followed curves of opposite directions, in other words. The
conclusion would be more credible if the correlation in
time were more positive. When this view is used to appraise
the situation, the inevitable conclusion is that prohibitions
are invariably leveled not merely at "sins" but at "sinful
pleasures." In other words, behaviors that appear to be
pleasurable to certain people are the ones prohibited.
Furthermore, in spite of the denial by others that they
might find pleasure in these activities themselves, there is
always the unspoken fear that they represent temptations
to others (their own children, for instance), thus acknowl-
edging a pleasurable component. Thus, labeling these

activities, through legal sanctions, as "bad" places them in the category desired—as something for people (one's own children, for example) to avoid, although they may be enjoyable.

Americans, however, are not the dour, sober people that these kinds of interpretations imply. Americans, unlike some of the very inhibited and conservative Europeans from whom they trace their ancestry, tend to be unusually spontaneous, given to merriment and celebration, usually optimistic, remarkably trustful of others, and very prone to personal pleasure. They tend to seek rather than avoid the forbidden, and are inclined to discredit the idea of living by prescriptions or rules. It would seem out of character for them, in this light, to legislate against something merely because it is a pleasure, even if it is sinful.

Another important element is characteristic of these prohibitions, however—the forbidden activities are also considered dangerous, to either the person pursuing them or to others. The traffic laws, especially the speed laws, would be of the same order—prohibitions against a potentially dangerous activity that people might be tempted to engage in because they expect to find pleasure in it. Thus, people boast of violating speed laws in much the same way that they once boasted of getting around the Volstead Act.

Until very recently, smoking had all the characteristics said to be true of the illegal vices, but there were no legal prohibitions against it. Now, for the first time, however, the threat of developing cancer and other diseases from smoking has introduced the element of danger, and the movement toward prohibition has therefore started, beginning with the enforced labeling of cigarettes as dangerous, then the prohibition against advertising on television. This time, the prohibition movement will be countered by strong vested commercial interests, and the resulting struggle will be interesting to watch. Practically all the arguments about legalizing or prohibiting drugs become debates over the question of danger.

It is time to point out that the danger issue is not enough to justify either a legal enforcement of prohibitions against a practice or the repeal of prohibitions against it. This issue begs the really important question—namely; What is the most workable way to control whatever dangers exist? As in the case of alcohol abuse, the experiment with national prohibition did nothing to eradicate the problem drinker; it only fixed to that danger the added one of poisoning people who were not problem drinkers. In other words, our many experiments with prohibitions have clearly shown that they have prevented all legitimate efforts to control the dangers, for prohibition inevitably means the absence of supervision, the absence of standards, and the impossibility of accurately knowing what is really going on.

For instance, one area in which society has had substantial success in dealing with dangers to people has been in the matter of industrial safety, and, as a result, industrial accidents and occupational diseases have declined significantly. This result was not accomplished by prohibiting a practice, but by imposing standards on the practice that took safety into account.

Once it is acknowledged that the vice laws are based not solely on the legal prohibition of pleasurable activities but on those pleasurable activities that are considered to be dangerous (rightly or wrongly), a degree of rationality can be found in the paradox we mentioned before—namely, the one that pointed out how the vice crusades seem to be directed solely toward getting a law passed, not toward enforcing it. In this case, it becomes easy for the American citizen to justify his indifference to enforcement, in spite of his vehement demand for the law. The law officially labels the practice in question as dangerous, and, because it is also supposed to be pleasurable, people are likely to try it. Now that it has been so labeled, the person who violates the law does so in peril of his own safety—he has been told not to do it; now if he does do it and suffers painful consequences, he has only himself to blame. With this kind of rationalization, it becomes the individual's own responsibility to enforce the law on himself, since it is his own safety that is at stake. When the practice also threatens other people's safety, then more interest in enforcement becomes evident—as in the case of the traffic laws. This view also can explain why Americans, during liquor prohibition days, supported the passage of the law but freely violated it themselves. In dealing with any dangerous practice, or one labeled as dangerous (driving a car too fast, for instance), most people will have a great deal more confidence in their own capacity to control the danger than they will have in the capacities of others to control themselves. It is no surprise, therefore, to find people failing to apply to themselves what they seek to impose on others.

To a large extent, the traffic laws are based on the wish, the hope, or the need to improve conditions of environmental safety. Only recently has there begun to grow a suspicion that their enforcement does not properly belong in the same category of responsibilities ordinarily assigned the police and the courts. This awareness has grown with the realization of the vast quantity of manpower used to enforce traffic laws. A recent survey of a large community, for instance, disclosed that 85 percent of all police activity, as measured by the distribution of man-hours among the various police tasks, was devoted to directing traffic, issuing parking tickets, trapping speeders, and appearing in court to testify on traffic violations. Meanwhile, in the same community, an untold list of unsolved crimes remained on the police books for want of sufficient manpower to investigate them. Typically, the traffic offender who is arrested is a somewhat careless but otherwise fairly respectable citizen, and not the dangerous criminal that society expects itself to be protected from by the police. Similarly, the violator of the vice prohibitions is typically a rather ordinary, non-criminal type of citizen (the real criminals working behind the scenes in the traffic end of vice are not the ones usually arrested). It would appear, in other words, that when traffic problems are included in the same category (of "safety regulations"), there is an enormous and expanding list of currently illegal acts occurring that deserve to be treated both philosophically and administratively in a different way than we expect true anti-crime efforts to be treated. If, in other words, the prevention of, apprehension of, or investigation of people who commit serious anti-social acts that threaten the lives and property of others are to be considered the proper function of the police and courts, then the safety regulations should properly be handled in a very different way, by different agencies. Public health programs are somewhat parallel examples wherein regulations and standards of health and safety are established and enforced with minimum police-type actions. The parallels between public health measures and the drug and alcohol problems are even more striking, in reality (not in practice, of course), than are the parallels between the drug and alcohol problems and crimes against persons and property.

A NEW LEGISLATIVE PROGRAM

Almost everyone with any significant degree of familiarity with the drug and alcohol problems will agree that changes in the existing system of laws and enforcement are in order. The opinions vary, however, from one extreme to the other on what these changes should be. The traditional policy originally and continuously advocated by those in sympathy with the Bureau of Narcotics has been to the effect that both laws and enforcement are essentially pointed in the right direction, except that more manpower is needed for enforcement, stricter punishments are required, and fewer civil rights safeguards should be extended to persons suspected of offenses. In accordance with this old philosophy, recent modifications have been on the order of permitting seizure and search without search warrants, thus raising in the eyes of others the specter of an impending police state. It has already become evident, in support of this position, that police make use of this freedom from restrictions on their activity to justify what would be otherwise illegal search and seizure, now justified on the grounds that drug possession is "suspected." The other extreme in the range of positions advocates the simple repeal of existing restrictions, either through formal repeal of laws, as has been done in the case of repealing anti-abortion laws, or by simply ignoring the prohibitions that are on the books. The possibility of having the restrictive laws declared unconstitutional, as has been the case with many of the anti-pornography laws, is another way of eliminating all restrictions, and seems more possible now than it ever seemed in the past. (Incidentally, a practical way of ensuring that this route will be followed would be to convince an enterprising legislator to add a simple amendment to anti-drug laws that would make cigarette smoking illegal. The reasons for prohibiting smoking are as sound as those against drug use, so such a move would be a logical one—except that it would almost certainly result in having the laws declared unconstitutional.)

Inasmuch as there are different sets of laws regulating

the different kinds of drugs, and certain aspects of the
drug problem vary according to the type of drug, some
degree of distinction must be drawn among them.

HARD NARCOTICS (HEROIN, ETC.)

The most disruptive aspect of the narcotic
(chiefly heroin) problem is the business of manufacturing
and distributing the drugs, inasmuch as organized crime
appears to be at the base of the business, and it has a very
strong vested interest in encouraging the spread of drug
abuse. Clearly, the objective in respect to legislation or
other government action should be to make the sale of
heroin unprofitable. The old promise of the Bureau of Narcotics was that the process of enforcing the anti-possession
laws against the heroin addict would have such a marked
deterrent effect on heroin use, and such a marked effect on
increasing costs, therefore decreasing profits, that this
method would serve the purpose. After several generations
of following this theory, it has been proven beyond any
shadow of doubt that it does not work. In other words,
profitability has not been diminished, and the increased
diligence in enforcement has only driven out the amateurs,
leaving the marketplace monopolized by the professionals
—and presumably the Mafia.

Profitability is determined by the difference in cost of
raw materials plus cost of manufacture and distribution,
on the one hand, and the selling price on the other. Following are some of the measures that have not been tried
but could have a devastating impact on reducing profitability:

1. Although the picture has been different in the past,
and could change in the future, the present traffic system

is approximately as follows: Both the legal and illicit supplies of raw materials (raw opium) come largely (80 to 90 percent) from a known and circumscribed poppy-growing area in Turkey. A recent estimate indicated that illicit smugglers buy the raw opium for about $35 per kilo, which is about double the official government price paid for the legal supplies. A kilo will yield a markup of from 20,000 to 50,000 times the wholesale price in the New York City retail market. Efforts to get the Turkish government to cooperate in curbing this illicit traffic have proven fruitless, but, in the very past few months, some promising signs have developed at the diplomatic level.

The raw opium is probably smuggled into neighboring Middle East countries (Lebanon, etc.) where it is converted into morphine by means of a relatively simple and inexpensive process. The morphine is then shipped to certain known plants in southern France where it is converted into heroin. It then apparently ends up in one or more Italian ports where it is then shipped to the United States, most often concealed in some legal cargo.

There are at least three, perhaps four, points in this distribution chain where simple American entrepreneurship (instead of fruitless diplomacy) could be effective in either drying up the supply or so drastically raising the wholesale price that the profit margin would be greatly reduced. The following, for instance, could be done on a somewhat straightforward business-like way by either U.S. government agents or by a designated private pharmaceutical company. The entire Turkish poppy crop could be bought by the mere process of out-bidding all the competition. The supplies thus bought would then be used by ethical American drug companies to meet the needs of the ethical traffic, and the balance (which would not be more than 10 percent of the total) would be destroyed. This would require a relatively small government subsidy, or the cost could be absorbed by a small increase, perhaps 15 percent, in the cost of legal narcotics. Instead of this procedure, but preferably in addition to it, the same tactic could be used in the Lebanese (or other Middle East) market where the morphine is manufactured, again buying up the entire supply by outbidding the competition. The practice could be repeated at Marseilles in order to control what supplies managed to get through the net and end up as heroin. Finally, in the American retail market, buying up any supplies that still got through, at a higher price than others are prepared to pay, would probably dry up virtually all the remainder. Once control over the raw materials and wholesale supply was established, then truly effective control could be imposed to modify the crop-growing practices of the poppy farmers. The illicit competition would rapidly lose its bargaining position as its capacity to obtain supplies was shut off, or as the cost of getting them was pushed to prohibitive levels and profits stopped rolling in.

2. Simultaneously, another, perhaps temporary, measure would be an almost certain guarantee of success. This measure would be one that, for a relatively short period of time, is needed to break up the traffic as it now exists, thus eliminating the retail market. Its utter simplicity and almost certain success are enough to recommend it. All that would be necessary would be to offer all existing heroin users a free supply. This could be done through the various medical channels available to the federal government, and on federal reservations (veterans hospitals, army, navy, airforce hospitals, public health hospitals). At these places, federal laws, not state and local laws, are in effect, and could provide the legal basis for the federal government to conduct a nationwide program without wait-

ing for cooperative state legislation. For practical purposes, the program might be conducted as follows: For a given six-month period, to coincide with the peak of activities undertaken to curb wholesale supplies, all heroin users in the country (perhaps 50,000 to 60,000) would be promised free, daily doses of narcotics for the rest of their lives (if necessary) if they registered during the six-month grace period, after which no one else could sign up (thus discouraging anyone from starting the habit). To be effective, nationwide news coverage of the entire plan would be necessary. Convincing guarantees of immunity from prosecution and a dependable source of supply for these registered heroin abusers also would be necessary to insure compliance.

3. A modification of the second step, which perhaps, would be more acceptable to the public, but by the same token less effective, would be to offer existing heroin abusers the methadone route. The weak point in this case would reside in the fact that, in order to gain public acceptance, the methadone route would likely be sold as a form of "treatment," and this myth might well be such as to mislead the abusers into failing to realize that methadone would do for them essentially whatever the heroin does. Thus, many of them might not be persuaded to cooperate.

4. A still further step might be taken to ensure public acceptance of the plan (hopefully, however, not necessary). This would consist of an offer to registered heroin abusers of a sanctuary on a federal reservation, thus both removing them from direct public visibility and placing them in a location where some degree of surveillance could be maintained.

5. Assuming that these steps were followed and carefully synchronized to achieve the maximum impact on the illicit market at all possible levels (wholesale and retail),

it is conceivable that the current profitability of drug trafficking could be almost totally wiped out. Perhaps most important, however, might be the resulting elimination of influences that would seek to recruit new users. For those few users who would still appear, programs could be adequately managed within standard medical channels without recourse to any public program.

MARIHUANA

The prospects of finding any feasible plan that could effectively eliminate the available supplies and sources of marihuana must be acknowledged to be nil. For instance, it is known that, in addition to the marihuana that is continuously imported from Mexico, the marihuana plant grows freely in at least thirty of the fifty states of the union. The current widespread use of marihuana has revealed that it is cheaply and easily obtainable in nearly all parts of the country. Furthermore, this state of free trade exists at a time in history when a massive, nationwide police effort is underway to curb it. Whereas heroin traffic seems to be almost entirely under the control of a single organization, which, therefore, could conceivably be put out of business, the marihuana traffic is maintained by countless people, including a very large number who are merely part-time amateurs. Furthermore, it also seems evident that profitability is not a major factor responsible for the establishment of supply channels. Rather, a common motive is to obtain supplies for personal use, with enough surplus to sell to defray the costs. Consequently, attacking the marihuana traffic with procedures designed primarily to reduce profitability will not be effective.

Painful though it might be to reach the conclusion, it is

now clearly evident that the only possible way of bringing any semblance of control to the marihuana problem now is to legalize it, and then control it through suitable licensing safeguards. Emphasis must be placed on the "now," for better long-term solutions can be devised through preventive, educational methods. At the present moment, however, considering the present generation of marihuana users, preventive education offers little prospect for results. The next generation should be the target of prevention.

Responsible people in influential circles who are deeply interested in reducing the scope and magnitude of the current drug problem must free themselves of many misleading arguments and assumptions in order to objectively appraise the best course of action to take. Clearly, many people who are influential and who previously were, perhaps, unalerted and uninvolved in the issues now see them as sufficiently urgent to demand remedial action. Perhaps for the first time, this applies to the President and the leaders in Congress. In 1968, President Nixon made campaign statements in keeping with his "law-and-order" theme that apparently endorsed the traditional hard line of the current punitive system. Soon after taking office, however, he was exposed to realities that considerably softened his attitude, but not to the point where any radical change in direction seems likely to emanate soon from the White House. Nevertheless, he appointed a Presidential Commission to study the question and recommend solutions. Even before this Commission arrived at the point of a final report, incidentally, it indicated that its findings would not be influenced by the President's previously stated hard line on the question. The first report was published in March 1972.

A fundamental assumption that many well-intentioned and responsible but unsophisticated political leaders have used as the basis of their policies toward marihuana is that it is dangerous. It leads to other crimes, the assumption goes, escalates to the use of hard drugs, and so restrictive and punitive procedures are called for to control it. Similarly, legalization of marihuana, according to this assumption, requires proof that it is a relatively "safe" drug. Nothing could be more misleading than this way of reasoning, for it accepts as fact something that has clearly been demonstrated to be far from fact—namely, that prohibition of sale and use (the current system) is, or could be, effective in keeping marihuana out of the hands of people who might be injured by it—if it is, indeed, dangerous. The truth is quite the opposite, for only through the rigorous controls that are feasible when it is legalized will this degree of safety be possible. Prohibition has always entailed losing control, not gaining it.

Another viewpoint that misleads the leaders in society who can be influential in either bringing about change or in maintaining the status quo is the kind that often comes from the proponents of legalization. These people are often verbal, though often abusive, anti-establishment types who advocate abolition of restrictions in order to stop the current harassment that threatens their own enjoyment of the drug. These people command too little sympathy from legislative and judicial leaders to have much more than the opposite effect from the one they seek. Thus, too many legislators, prosecutors, and judges have been unwittingly forced into the position of opposing legalization because they are not in sympathy with its advocates as people. Thus, a situation is created much like the one that existed during liquor prohibition when the bootleggers and the do-gooders typically banded together to forestall repeal, with the bootleggers' most persuasive argument against repeal (to protect their illicit business) being public statements in favor of it.

The government authorities who are concerned with finding better solutions than those now in force need not abandon the concept of *control* in order to consider the possibilities of legalization. Instead, they must confront themselves with the question: What is the best way to obtain and maintain some reasonable degree of control? To answer this question, it is necessary to: (1) agonizingly reappraise our past efforts and admit that they did not work, and (2) look to other areas where government has been successful in bringing some social danger under reasonable control, and consider what lessons might be learned from these experiences. For instance, in those parts of the country where the civil rights of minority groups were once seriously infringed, but where substantial progress against segregation and discrimination has been achieved, something of value can be learned. The progress did not come about by passing laws prohibiting schools, buses, or restaurants where some of the old evils were practiced. Industrial safety and occupational health hazards have been sharply reduced in many areas, but not by closing down factories. Much progress has been made in improving the safety of automobiles but not by prohibiting automobiles. In nearly every case in which steady improvement in health and safety has occurred, progress has come about through direct federal government participation in planning, in design, in research, and in granting subsidies. Perhaps the example that most closely parallels the current drug problem but that has improved immeasurably is the field of food and drug inspection. Since 1910, when the Pure Food and Drug Acts were passed, there has been steady improvement in the degree of consumer safety in the field of food, cosmetics, over-the-counter drugs, prescription drugs, and food additives. An indication of the degree of improvement was recently evidenced when a

single case of botulinus poisoning was traced to a single
can of contaminated soup. The remarkable thing about
the incident escaped the news media, for it was the rarity
of its occurrence today as compared with its very common
occurrence a couple of generations ago that made the incident so remarkable. Furthermore, in spite of how often
contamination used to occur, it was heretofore uncommon
for the food processor, who was then responsible, to suffer
any serious consequences. On the recent occasion of the
tainted soup, however, the company responsible went
bankrupt—because of only one, single mistake—one out
of millions of non-mistakes. Again, however, the advances
made in the safety of food and other ingested substances
did not come about by merely prohibiting them, but by
establishing effective standards, and with a very minimum
of police action to support them.

The current problem that is most nearly identical to the
marihuana problem is that of alcohol abuse. They are
alike in the following ways: (1) It has already been clearly
established that it is impossible to eliminate the sources
of supply, for both are very easily manufactured, and both
are very widely desired by people in all strata of society.
Therefore, regardless of what system is put into effect, it
must start off with the realization that a lot of people are
going to want whatever it is that is prohibited, and most
of them are going to get it. (2) It is now clear in both
cases, although once clear only for alcohol, that both relatively reasonable and responsible people, as well as others
not so mature, have been using them and probably will
continue to use them. In other words, in neither case is
the use confined to people who constitute some sort of
social or psychological problem. (3) It is equally clear,
and because of the same factors, that in the hands of many
people (responsible and mature people), both substances

are safe in the way they are used—probably safer, in fact, than tobacco smoking. By the same token, it also follows that the use of either substance by the irresponsible, immature people can be dangerous, both to themselves and to others (via auto accidents while under the influence, for instance). (4) Finally, the immediate, intoxicating effect of either marihuana or alcohol is essentially indistinguishable (all poetry to the contrary notwithstanding), and this immediate effect is a by-product of (3). That is to say, the effect on reasonable people is the familiar one most people experience when they enjoy a glass of beer or a cocktail. On the other kinds of people, the effects are not so different, but these people are much more likely to use too much, too often, and at the wrong time or place, and the effects can thus become a problem.

Because the alcohol and the marihuana problems are so nearly identical, it would make good sense to establish a new system of control to include the two problems in the same program and procedures. That is not to say that marihuana might be sold and distributed as alcoholic beverages are now, but that both be subjected to a system of manufacture, sale, and distribution—through the same channels—that includes both but which is an improvement over the present system. At least two glaring evils now occur commonly in the alcohol distribution system and are fully correctable. (Britain has recently, for instance, made advances along these lines.) Liquor store dealers and bars that sell liquor by the drink now knowingly sell to people who are either (1) obviously intoxicated already, or (2) about to drive an automobile while intoxicated. These evils can be stopped quickly and decisively by granting authority as well as a suitable set of rewards and punishments for salesmen to use in determining to whom they may sell liquor, and by holding them responsible for damages incurred (while driving an auto, for instance) as a result of anything they have done to knowingly contribute to someone's state of intoxication.

In other words, the present system of alcohol distribution must first be improved in order to reduce the known and obvious dangers that it now breeds. Second, it is proposed that marihuana be sold and distributed through the same channels as liquor, with the same licenses, taxes, and with the same controls.

Furthermore, another new move would also be in order and would be so eminently sensible, if followed, that no reasonable arguments could be found to oppose it. It would be exceedingly fitting that a certain percentage (say 20 percent) of all the taxes collected from both alcohol and marihuana be categorically retained in a special fund in the federal Treasury to finance research, public education programs, and treatment centers for drug and alcohol problems. The objective of relating the revenues from one to the expenditures for the other as a fixed percentage would be to guarantee that if the use (therefore taxes) went up, then money to pay for preventive programs would also increase, but, otherwise, if use (therefore taxes) declined, then money to pay for preventive programs would also appropriately decline.

PRESCRIPTION DRUGS
(TRANQUILIZERS, SYNTHETIC
NARCOTICS, SEDATIVES, ANALGESICS)

Most, but not all, of the responsibility for bringing the current excesses in prescription drug use under control belongs to the medical profession. Fainthearted efforts in that direction have just begun to appear within the hallowed circles of the American Medical Association.

More pressure on physicians than the AMA typically exerts is necessary in order to make this move a decisive one. Contrary to what is commonly believed, physicians (in their individual practices) are not particularly sensitive to advice and policies emanating either from their own national societies or from government agencies (such as the Federal Drug Administration). Instead, physicians are most responsive to the following two sources of pressure: (1) malpractice suits (usually initiated by enterprising attorneys rather than by disgruntled patients), and (2) the wishes, the demands, and the preferences of the public as the public is represented by their patients. At the present time, there is no warning list of malpractice suit decisions against physicians for having prescribed *unnecessary* medication (capable of leading to drug abuse). The closest type of suit has been against physicians for unexpected toxic side-effects of drugs—suits that perhaps more properly should be directed against the drug manufacturer. Furthermore, there has not been, until now, even a whisper of protest from the public at large against the common practice of over-medication. The reasons for the absence of protest are rather obvious, for the typical over-medicated patient is the one who has himself (more often, herself) insisted on more drugs from the physician, and the latter has complied, thus sharing the responsibility, but not the blame.

There are only one hundred medical schools in the United States. It would not be an insuperable task to mobilize this relatively small group of otherwise highly responsible people to launch a new and massive attack at the training level against excessive medication. A similar step has recently been inaugurated and has proved to be quite successful. This move, which started only about fifteen years ago, is aimed at stopping unnecessary operations in hospitals. A measure of the success of this move is the fact

that the number of appendectomies (one of the formerly
common unnecessary operations) has dropped by half. The
method by which this step was accomplished was to set
up in each hospital a review committee to evaluate the
pathology found in each operation and to censure physicians who performed too many operations that disclosed
no pathology.

It would probably also be effective if a concerted effort
to highlight the existence of excessive prescribing were
made painfully manifest through a number of malpractice
suits. If a number of these suits were instituted, particularly after the medical schools of the country began a new
program to eliminate this evil, thus giving it the status of
an unaccepted medical procedure, physicians certainly
would be forced to consider them before they acted. Individual physicians who are in private practice and appear
to be well trained and highly responsible will generally
admit (to another physician, not to an outsider) that excessive prescribing is, in fact, a most prevalent evil. Nevertheless, these very physicians often are guilty of the same
practice, and sometimes in spite of the fact that they are
in the process of teaching students and interns to do otherwise. It is more than likely that a large majority of physicians would welcome a nation-wide program to which all
physicians are ostensibly subscribing to bring about a reduction in their own use of excessive prescriptions. In
other words, they apparently need, and would probably
respond to, a face-saving way of actually doing what their
conscience and training dictate, even though they have,
heretofore, been doing the opposite.

Not all the prescription drugs manufactured in the country are under the control of physicians. The manufacturers
and the pharmacists also have a great deal of control over
where the drugs are channeled and it is clear that the
only legal channel—through physicians' prescriptions—

does not account for anything like the total of all drugs manufactured and sold. There are leaks in the distribution system that can be plugged, and the Federal Drug Administration has the authority to do this. The FDA, however, relies on voluntary compliance and is limited in its manpower. The voluntary system probably works quite well for the well-known ethical manufacturers, but, unfortunately, there are also a number of wholesalers and distributors who are not ethical and who do not comply with the regulations and accounting procedures. This part of the business has been overlooked in the current control system, and the flaw needs to be corrected. An effective threat that could be used to guarantee compliance would be to require that the amount of all drugs manufactured must correspond with the number prescribed, and if the figures did not balance, then physicians would be required to purchase the drugs directly from the manufacturer without going through any middlemen (and at less cost). It is clearly the middlemen who divert these drugs from legal channels, and the ethical ones can police the business effectively if the alternative is to lose their share of the business.

OVER-THE-COUNTER DRUGS (MEDICATIONS, SUCH AS ASPIRIN, THAT CAN BE PURCHASED WITHOUT A PRESCRIPTION BY THE PUBLIC)

The greatest danger of the over-the-counter drugs is not what they contain. For the past twenty to thirty years, the restrictions imposed by the FDA have gradually eliminated from these "patent medicines" nearly all drugs that have any effect at all, except aspirin and alcohol. It is, instead, the advertising of these drugs that does the harm. The clever innuendo of the sophisticated television commercial is careful not to make any actual claim that cannot be supported, but nevertheless, it succeeds in creating the impression in the public mind that they have powerful and nearly magical properties. The tremendous profit potential of this business has created powerful lobbies that have so far prevented any but the most trivial inroads on their freedom to exploit the public. Probably the most effective way to neutralize such advertising and lobbying is not through more action on the part of the Federal Trade Commission (the usual route followed), but through a counter, public education program. As recommended for the alcohol and marihuana problems, it would make sense to levy a tax on these over-the-counter drugs, the proceeds of which would be used exclusively to finance public education campaigns.

CONTROL EFFECTIVENESS

There are certain considerations that are generally overlooked when legislative or administrative control systems are designed to limit or restrict human behavior. The effectiveness of a new control system depends not only on the activity in question being controllable, but also on certain characteristics of the population concerned. It is never enough that a prohibitive rule or law with accompanying penalties be established in order to assure a degree of compliance that could be considered satisfactory. Other influences must also be brought to bear to enforce the provisions—and not the least of these is public opinion. In order to rally support for the new control system, the population whose activities are meant to be restricted or controlled must be one that is responsive to public opinion. This quality would not ordinarily apply to criminals, for instance, but could apply to licensed professional people. Furthermore, the controls themselves must be designed to conform to common and prevailing attitudes on the part of the public.

Examples of the above constraints would be as follows: (1) Controlling alcohol or drug use by forbidding adolescents to use them is impossible, even if public opinion might favor it. (2) Forbidding all people to drink or use drugs will inevitably fail to win the support of public opinion. (3) Restrictions designed to curb profitable activities of international organized crime through ordinary police work and ordinary legal sanctions, as is now the case with narcotics traffic, are doomed to failure simply because the target population is more adept at their business than the police are at theirs. (4) The requirement that physicians and pharmacists exercise more responsibility and diligence in the disbursement of drug prescriptions is feasible because these professionals will be responsive, if they have participated and been consulted in drafting the plan. (5) Sanctions against bartenders, for instance, for serving drinks to people already intoxicated, or to those about to drive a car, are likely to be endorsed by public opinion because the public sees its own safety at stake. (6) Ethical manufacturers, but not a host of other businesses dealing in the manufacture and distribution of drugs and alcohol, are responsive to clear-cut public opinion when its effect is such that the public image of the business is either enhanced or degraded.

An age-old adage that applies to the likelihood of a given law or rule being complied with states that a law is enforceable only if a very large majority of the population already behaves in accordance with its provisions, even before it has been legislated. For instance, an anti-birth-control law might have worked in the nineteenth century, but could not in the twentieth century because now most people would violate it almost as a matter of course. Regulations, in other words, inevitably are imposed by the majority on the minority, and are effective to the degree to which the majority outnumbers and influences the minority.

Another element to take into account in regulating behavior is the access that society has to other facilities or other well-established controls that might be used to control the activity in question. For example, society has certain facilities concerning automobile driving (licenses, highways, state police, and so on), and certain established controls over the use of these facilities. Incorporating into existing controls certain standards of sobriety, for example, is more feasible and more likely to win the approval of public opinion than would, for instance, prohibitions against public drunkenness, simply because additional incentives (desire to retain drivers' privileges) exist. Already a great deal has been accomplished along these lines, but lessons from the newly inaugurated British system might also be learned (alcohol-breath test requirement for drivers). Another interesting device that has been suggested would also be worth studying. This idea is to rule that alcoholics and so-called drug addicts cannot be held liable for debts incurred through use of credit cards. The effect of such a rule would be to require those passing out credit cards to assure themselves that alcoholics and so-called drug addicts do not get them, and it would also have the peculiar effect of requiring the subject to prove himself an alcoholic or drug addict in order to be immune to judgments for non-payment of debts. It seems unlikely that such a rule would ever be put into effect, but the possibilities are interesting, at least, to contemplate.

Chapter
11

SOLUTIONS:
PREVENTION PROGRAMS

Iᶠ any lesson is to be learned from medicine and public health that might be applied to the drug and alcohol problem it is that the best investments can be made at the preventive level rather than the curative level. Even the most effective efforts to cure the current problem by attacking the use and abuse of ingested substances can, at best, arrest the growth of the problem, but cannot wipe it out. If, however, effective programs are designed to keep new generations of potential users and abusers from taking up drugs and alcohol, eventually the problem can be solved—but only in the fairly distant future.

Above all, a rather radical cultural transformation must occur if drastic improvements are to result. Extremely pervasive public attitudes and concepts must be changed in the direction of disenchanting people about the magic of chemistry. It is hopeless to expect that those people now deeply imbued with these beliefs will be likely to abandon them. It is not so hopeless, however, to disillusion new generations before they have become indoctrinated.

Long-range public education programs would not properly begin by beaming the message to the actual target population (children and youth), but, first, to those professional people and leaders in society who control the instruments of power that influence youth. Above all, it would be important to plan a long-range program that sets out first to enlist the cooperation of those people in society who are most responsive to social pressures, have the most obvious vested interests in preserving the social system, and are most in tune with established channels of communication. Some feeble, and expensive, attempts are now being made to directly influence the youthful drug culture, but clearly have the effect only of polarizing the "good guy-bad guy" segments of the population, thus serving to encourage rebellion against the establishment.

CLUE TO POSSIBLE ATTITUDES OF FUTURE PHYSICIANS TO MARIHUANA USE

The authors questioned 1,063 future physicians at four medical schools in different geographic regions of the United States concerning their attitudes toward marihuana and its use. Their results indicated that past use of *cannabis* ranged from 17 per cent of the students at one school to 70 per cent at another. Over 500 students in the four schools had used marihuana at least once, and 114 said they had used the drug more than 100 times. More than 300 said they were using *cannabis* currently.

Author's summary of: Marijuana Use by Medical Students, *M. R. Lipp, S. G. Benson, and Z. Tainter,* American Journal of Psychiatry, *August, 1971.*

EFFECTIVE PUBLIC EDUCATION

New preventive programs that stress public education will do well to take into account recent successes and failures. Hopefully, both the successes and failures will contain useful information for designing new programs meant to bring about a substantial change in the behavior and attitudes of the general public. Confining our attention to the present century, which has been marked by the extensive development of public education media, the following might be cited as examples of successes:

SUCCESSES

1. An area quite relevant to the issue of drug and alcohol problems, in one sense at least, is the health consciousness and sophistication of the population. There would appear to be no doubt that a very large majority of the adult population now possesses a level of health awareness and health knowledge that directs them to generally sound decisions concerning their own health care as well as public health matters. At the beginning of this century, on the other hand, quackery was practiced on an equal par and was just as respected as scientific medicine. People by the hundreds of thousands were contracting and dying of illnesses that were then preventable, while innumerable curable conditions failed to receive the effective treatment then available because of ignorance or indifference. Some facts that reveal the changes that have occurred include the following: the percentage of babies born in hospitals has steadily risen from a very tiny fraction of the total babies born at the beginning of the century to nearly 100 percent today; the degree of patronage of quacks and the general respect accorded them has fallen to a point where this is now a relatively inconsequential problem; child-

OVER-MEDICATED AMERICA

Miller estimates that self-medication with over-the-counter drugs cost the American public $2 billion in 1969, and that 200 different drugs are the principal ingredients in 100,000 commercial preparations. Of these, only 15 percent were rated as effective remedies by the Federal Drug Administration.

By means of various estimates, Miller concludes that the typical physician spends only seventeen minutes with each patient per visit, and comes to rely heavily on a protocol for terminating this brief encounter in a way that satisfies the patient. Writing a prescription serves this purpose, and this factor tends to lead to wide use of unnecessary medications.

Miller further points out a probable factor that prevents patients from complaining about the system. Frequently, the cost of the (unnecessary?) prescription is weighed against the cost of losing time from work, and, in this context, the cost does not appear to be as excessive as it might otherwise seem.

Author's summary of: The Over-Medicated Society: Forces in the Marketplace for Medical Care, *Charlotte Muller*, Science, *May 5, 1972.*

hood immunization against preventable communicable disease is almost universal today; there tends to be widespread interest and very substantial respect for the scientific advances made in medicine—these are considered highly newsworthy, and the general public tends to keep quite up to date on what is going on in the field.

The factors responsible for the vast progress made in

health education in this century begin with the all-important fact that, simultaneously, one life-saving discovery after another was being made available to the public. Physicians and hospitals tremendously improved their standards of care and life expectancy advanced, for the average person, from fifty to seventy years. These accomplishments, however, were not enough to disseminate the extensive knowledge about health matters that accumulated and the health consciousness that developed—these required public education. The principal focus of interest that led to the increased knowledge involved the issue of pregnancy and child care. Clearly, the young mother or expectant mother is the family member who becomes most intensely interested in the subject and absorbs most of the knowledge that is readily available. As a result, the numerous women's magazines have been a leading source of information. Typically, the young mother becomes the custodian

ON CURRENT ANTI-DRUG CAMPAIGNS

A director of a drug clinic in Boston, Dr. G. E. Davidson, commented in an interview that the current program of the federal government is "inaccurate" and made up of ineffective "sermonizing." He cited the typical example of a well-known athlete in a televised publicity release advising youngsters to "get a kick out of driving through the line instead of using drugs." The drug expert commented that, "certainly the kids at risk are not the great athletes in the world and they are not playing games with anybody. How can they identify with a well-known pro football player?"

Author's summary of a U.P.I. news release, October, 1971.

of the family's health and influences the health practices
and knowledge of the rest of the family. An important
factor in this respect has been the trend in this century
toward smaller and smaller families, leaving more and
more of the young mother's energies and time available to
care for her fewer children. The mere fact that the trend
during this century has been toward a planned family,
with the parents deciding when and how many children
there will be, makes deliberate planning and preparation
through pre-natal care and pre-natal education likely.

2. Not far removed from the developments pointed out
in (1) is the increasing safety consciousness of the public
—safety being comparable in many ways to the problem
of alcohol and drug use. The increasing power of machines
of this century to maim and kill has had a great deal to
do with alerting the public to the need for safety. Illus-
trative of the great changes that have taken place in public attitudes toward safety are the ways we now build and
equip our home, farm, and factories. The typical American
today can quickly detect numerous examples of poor safety
practices in old abandoned places of work and living, but
in those days, the now-evident hazards were largely regarded as unavoidable. An important and essential change
in values occurred somewhere along the way when attention to safety—even publicly admitted fear of danger—
stopped being regarded as something effeminate. Unions
have done quite a bit to instill safety concepts in the business world by including safety provisions in shop contracts.
Again, as in the case of general health sophistication, the
focus of attention on little children in the home has highlighted for parents the necessity of being alert to safety.
Nevertheless, in spite of the progress that has been made,
safety hazards still plague society. Clearly, the remaining
safety problems are attributable to the accelerating rate

PRESCRIPTION DRUG PROMOTION

In testimony before the Senate Subcommittee on Monopoly, a psychiatrist from the State University of New York at Syracuse charged that the U.S. is in the throes of a "drug pandemic." He criticized physicians for using drugs as a panacea for "life situations and problems beyond the traditional medical and psychiatric concepts of illness or disease." He said of his colleagues, "prone to drug dependence ourselves, we have *turned on* our client: white, middle-class America—and the kids come tripping after."

He went on to warn that it may be too late to reclaim "the national medical societies from their dependence on income from drug sources. He pointed to the AMA as being in "a virtual partnership with the drug industry," because much of the organization's income comes from drug sources.

Author's summary of a news item in the newsletter of the American Psychiatric Association, October, 1971.

at which technology advances, and with it the power of machines to do harm. In spite of man's awareness of the danger, machines continually outdistance the human operator's ability to control them. If, for example, the same kinds of automobiles were being used now as were available in 1925, chances are we would have a very favorable automobile safety record. No sooner, however, does a generation of drivers learn to master one level of technology than technology takes a quantum jump forward, requiring that new skills be learned. Nevertheless, the safety consciousness of Americans is strikingly keener than that of most Europeans, a phenomenon that is evident when one compares the attitudes of foreign auto drivers with those of American drivers.

Probably the single, most effective educational device for promoting safety consciousness in the United States has been the use (and abuse) of the negligence suit in court. It is rare for people to be prosecuted or even publicly censured because of poor safety habits and practices. It is, however, very common for people to be keenly aware of the possibilities of being threatened with a civil negligence suit. Hence, nearly all citizens, both in their private lives and in the business world, carry one or more kinds of insurance to protect themselves against claims made in these suits. This would include, for instance, the workmen's compensation insurance carried by employers and the malpractice insurance carried by physicians.

MARIHUANA: ALCOHOL PROBLEMS COMPARED

"The federal marihuana commission, still months away from its first formal report, is proceeding on the hypothesis that drunks are a far worse social problem than pot smokers.

"We do know this, the most severe drug abuse problem we've got in the United States is alcohol," the commission executive director, Michael Sonnenreich, told the Associated Press.

"President Nixon has said he will ignore any recommendations to legalize marihuana use, but the commission chairman, Raymond P. Shafer, Republican former governor of Pennsylvania, says Nixon's views won't influence the commission."

From an Associated Press news release, Washington, D.C., September, 1971.

Also, the bravado and foolishness that might be associated with any practice that is clearly unsafe no longer is accorded the attention it might have drawn at one time, or that it might attract in some other cultures. Only in the very immature auto driver, for instance, is this kind of behavior likely to be regarded as bravado and assertiveness. Almost everyone else looks on it for what it is—foolish.

Public education on matters of safety over the past seventy years did not involve any massive crusade. Instead, the efforts have been subdued, and largely indirect. They were indirect in the sense that the teaching of safety practices came to be intimately tied into the teaching of how to live with, use, and operate modern technology. In other words, safety consciousness in America has become largely a by-product of the American citizen's mastery of technology. As an example, one of the items of interest uppermost in the minds of citizens who were witnessing our recent man-in-space and man-on-the-moon ventures was the question of safety. The one great tragedy in the space program was the accidental fire during a simulated Apollo flight that killed three astronauts. The National Safety Council has been instrumental in keeping interest in safety alive, but possibly more effective has been the National Underwriters Association, which determines safety standards for insurance purposes.

3. Although its social value might not be commensurate with the results we have just outlined, another outstanding success in public education during this century can be cited. This development started on a large scale only as recently as the 1920s, but it is responsible for vast changes in the American scene. Primarily through advertising, but also aided considerably by the movies, radio, and television, American women have been made self-conscious about their appearance, self-conscious to the point where

1971 DRUG CONSUMPTION IN NEW YORK STATE

525,000 New York State residents were currently using, regularly, a minor tranquilizer, such as Miltown, Valium, or Librium.

377,000 persons were using barbiturates at least once a month.

225,000 persons were regularly using a drug containing amphetamines.

485,000 persons were regularly using marihuana; half of them were using it on the job.

Sales workers were the most frequent users among occupational categories.

Housewives were the most frequent users among groups of occupational and non-occupational categories.

41,000 persons were using heroin at least six times a month.

From a survey by the New York Narcotics Addiction Control Commission on the extent of current use of "dangerous drugs," November, 1971.

the typical American woman, beginning at a very early age and continuing almost until death, is preoccupied with how she smells, how her hair looks, how her clothes are cut, and how white her teeth are. Female attractiveness is no longer solely a function of wealth or social class, and even age itself no longer means loss of attractiveness. On the other side of the coin, huge new industries have risen and prospered both to exploit this self-consciousness and to cultivate it even further in new directions.

The success of this advertising promotion can probably be attributed to the fact that several related events occurred almost simultaneously. The new freedom of women after World War I was a prime mover, but at the same time, economic prosperity, the rapid evolution of the automobile, the swift spread of popularity of the movies, and the acceptance of, and technology for, birth control occurred at the same time. All were related both in time and in public attitude to the advertising message that was leveled at women during the 1920s, apparently encouraging them to seize their rights and their pleasures and heightening their self-consciousness. Whether real or manufactured by advertising, public opinion forced women into the beauty mold. In other words, by not buying certain products, a woman risked being ostracized by society because of body odor, dull teeth, or general lack of stylishness.

NEW MOVES TO CURB EXCESSIVE PRESCRIPTIONS

Amphetamine Use Curbed in England

"Many physicians in England and Scotland, like their counterparts in the U.S., have voluntarily stopped prescribing amphetamines in an effort to curb abuses of the drugs.

According to a *British Medical Journal* editorial, the action by the physicians has resulted in a gratifying reduction in the amount of amphetamine drugs prescribed.

The success to date, the journal noted, has made many physicians 'ask themselves whether other potential drugs of dependence at present being prescribed without much thought could not also be exposed to similar careful scrutiny.' "

From the AMA News, *August, 1971.*

A measure of how far the American woman has gone in the directions mentioned, and the universal acceptance of this as good, is revealed by the devastating public censure leveled at the modern hippie girl who holds these values in contempt.

These three "successes" are not meant to make up a comprehensive list, but are only examples to show what can happen to produce drastic changes in the behavior of millions of people. There have also been failures, and a few of these might be mentioned to balance the picture:

FAILURES

1. Perhaps the most serious failure in public education in the United States has been lack of success in getting our citizens to take the kind of interest in government and politics, and to participate, in ways which would insure both good government and respect for government. One of the outstanding measures of this lack of success is the generally poor showing, in numbers, of the electorate at the polls. Even much less democratic societies than ours muster a very much higher percentage of the total vote on election day than we do. In addition, public indifference accounts for a great deal of the mismanagement that is prevalent in government, and, even more serious, the corruption that often exists. The low level of respect in which politicians are held by Americans screens out our best qualified candidates and attracts the very kinds whose performances feed the disrespect.

For the most part, efforts to educate the citizenry in responsible participation in government have been confined to the school system, and perhaps this is why the job has been done so badly. None of the "successes," on the other hand, can be traced to efforts made in the schools. An over-all review of the history of what our public schools

ON LEGALIZATION OF MARIHUANA

"Legalization of marihuana would create a serious abuse problem in the United States. The current (illicit) use of marihuana . . . is not commonly of high potency, and street samples are sometimes heavily adulterated with inert materials. . . . If all controls were eliminated, potent preparations would dominate the legal market, even as they now are beginning to appear on the illicit market. If the potency of the drug were legally controlled predictably there would be a market for the more powerful legal forms."

From the report of the American Medical Association and National Research Council, 1968

have tried to teach, outside of academic subjects, indicates, in fact, that Americans typically leave in the schools whatever they learn there, and do not apply it outside.

In contrast, the British maintain a tradition of interest in government and a respect for the system (including the laws) that is much more self-fulfilling than ours. The British pay close attention to what their government does, and the government, in turn, tends to be less inclined to be swayed by passing fashions and more inclined to take the long-term view. This approach tends to discourage demagoguery and command respect, which tends to attract better qualified leaders.

2. Another eminent lack of success that only recently has begun to creep into the awareness of Americans is our failure to abandon violent means of solving problems. In the 1970s, America seems no closer than it was in seemingly more barbaric times in the past to first exhaust all other alternatives before resorting to force. Instead, the use

THE HIDDEN PERSUADERS AND THE DRUG CULTURE

Nicholas Johnson, member of the Federal Communications Commission and a leading critic of the broadcast industry, said yesterday home remedy commercials should be banned from the airwaves because they add to the drug menace.

"If we are really serious about dealing with drug abuse in this country," Johnson told a Senate committee, "let's move now to stop the television pushers."

Johnson, also an outspoken critic of the FCC itself, appeared with six fellow comissioners before a subcommittee examining over-the-counter sales of medicines, particularly pain killers and mood drugs such as tranquilizers, sleeping aids, pep pills and antidepressants.

In urging that such commercials be banned, Johnson said those who promote them should be asked "personally how they can justify what they do—whether it is a network president, a product manufacturer, an advertising agency executive, or a federal communication commissioner."

Charging that the commercials promote the use of drugs and drug abuse, Johnson said, "the advertising is positively harmful and serves no useful purpose."

The committee, chaired by Sen. Gaylord Nelson, D-Wis., heard medical testimony last spring that such drugs are not as effective as advertised and that commercials promoting them are not only frequently deceptive but foster "drug culture."

From a U.P.I. news release, Washington, D.C., September, 1971.

of force appears too often to be the first choice. Hence, campus violence, big-city riots, prison massacres, murders, and the pursuit of senseless wars continue unabated, in spite of an apparent advance in the level of civilization. A not inconsiderable factor probably responsible for this warped social phenomenon might be Americans' well-known tendency to deal directly, rather than indirectly with problems. Perhaps more significant, however, is a prevailing myth held by Americans of their moral righteousness and their unchallenged faith in the good intentions supposedly underlying their violent methods. Our history books point out that America has never been "wrong" nor even "defeated," although the exorbitant costs of victory are rarely mentioned.

It might be argued that this example does not represent a failure of public education on the grounds that no effort was ever made to educate the public to the costs of violence and to the desirability of first examining other alternatives. In one sense, this is true—if the problem were accepted as stated. On the other hand, our schools, our government, and our public news media are forever stressing that the United States is the greatest "freedom loving" country in the world, and that we are obliged to ensure "peace" and "freedom," or "law and order" everywhere. By extension, then, the violence that results from our internal or external "peace-keeping" efforts is "forced" on us by the "unreasonableness" of our opponents, and is not of our own choosing. Thus, Americans can blindly impose forceful restraints on others in the interests of "freedom," or kill others, if necessary, to "keep the peace." Until ten years ago, anyone who pointed out the obvious contradictions in this kind of reasoning would have been branded unpatriotic. Today this mythology is being challenged, but in the face of massive resistance from the established order.

3. Another public education failure that suddenly appears to be on the verge of being changed to a success is the conservation issue. In the past, rather than thinking and planning ahead, we consumed, wasted, and destroyed our irreplaceable resources without regard for the future. Our current awareness of the problems of air and water pollution, of dwindling fuel and mineral supplies, of disappearing natural beauty, might turn out to be, as some alarmists predict, too late. At least a change has occurred in public attitudes. What most people now active in the movement are unaware of, however, is how long it has taken to become aware. Public alarm did not develop until the problems became almost unmanageable. Perhaps our past apathy can be attributed to its apparent conflict between conservation and other national goals and experiences. Until this very moment in history, we have assumed that expansion and "progress" in all areas of national life and the economy were both desirable and inevitable. We have also realized enormous profits (short-term, at least) from the wastefulness of such activities as war. In these contexts, conservation seemed to connote an un-modern, un-technological, impractical approach and an immediate impediment to prosperity. Not until today have these concepts been re-examined in the context of their basic assumptions, and a sounder, long-range policy begun to emerge.

Lessons to be Learned

A prevailing theme in modern American history, and one fundamental to an understanding of how our country works, is the role of fashion in determining public behavior. In each of the examples mentioned, for example, it was the appearance, or the non-appearance, of popular fashions that had a lot to do with new concepts, attitudes, and practices sweeping the country, or failing to gain acceptance. Elaborate and well-greased machinery is always available to mobilize massive public education efforts to convert a passing fancy, an obscure movement or philosophy, or a different status symbol to a nationwide fashion. New fashions gain momentum if they are profitable to large business enterprises, for the financing of their sustained programming thereby becomes guaranteed. Similarly, it is difficult to establish a new fashion that conflicts with the vested commercial interests of powerful business enterprises, especially if these enterprises control news and advertising media. In some instances, there is profit to be made, but the possibilities are not immediately self-evident, so that the development of a new fad is gradual, much like the way the conservation–anti-pollution crusade has developed. Initially, big business resisted the conservation movement because it looked like it would be enormously expensive to implement, but as the profit potential in conservation became gradually more apparent, even big business got behind the movement, although usually by advising others what to do, rather than by taking any action.

Another quality important to the development of a new fashion is the public's readiness to accept it. People are less likely to jump on another bandwagon if a new one has just passed through. In other words, timing is important and critical. One side of the fashion coin is the great momentum a fashion can develop once it is launched, but the other side is the readiness of people to forget it after it has been around for a while.

Another characteristic element in American behavior is our readiness to join crusades that pit the "good" against the "bad," particularly if the bad can be pictured as somehow undeserving of the "made in America" label—that is, somehow in conflict with American tradition and mythology. It is also evident, at least heretofore, that Americans do not seem to be very responsive to efforts to educate them when such efforts are labeled as "education." Direct efforts by government agencies to educate the public seem only to inspire citizens to look for loopholes. Note, for example, the public indifference to government warnings of the harmful effects of smoking. In contrast, advertisers many times each day warn people they might have a bad odor and in response manage to induce millions of citizens to march dutifully to the drug store to buy a deodorant!

More than most older Americans care to admit, the American culture is, above all, a youth culture. Our heroes are the young, the daring, the romantic—not the old and wise. Our pleasant memories tend to be those of our youth; our personal investments are heavily weighted in favor of the young, and the very alarms and hostilities we see expressed toward certain young people today show how vividly they command our attention.

In summary, then, some of the elements that it would be wise to take into account in designing a new campaign of public education, in this case, one designed to reduce the severity of the drug and alcohol problem through preventive measures, include the following: (1) Capitalize on the tendency for Americans to seize on new fashions. To establish a new fashion—one, for instance, in which drugs and alcohol play a less conspicuous part in national life—it would help to build in a profit motive for compliance, and to be careful in timing the campaign. (2) In addition, new sets of status symbols that equate desirable American virtues with the rational use or avoidance of alcohol and drugs need to be invented. Instead, for example, of equating the ability to consume large quantities of liquor with manliness (as before), it might be equated with poor automobile driving or a poor credit rating, thus discrediting it. (3) Inevitably, it would be the youth of the country who will become the target for preventive programs. Efforts to educate them on the grounds that drugs or alcohol are immoral will only make their use sound more exciting. It might be more effective to relate the avoidance of these substances to qualities that make the young seem superior to older people who are still addicted to them, superior in the sense of being more insightful, more responsible, or more intelligent, but not more moral.

Clearly, one of the apparent obstacles to launching a public education program like the one just outlined appears to be the unlikelihood of making sobriety profitable, thus counteracting the present situation wherein non-sobriety is profitable to many powerful vested interests. We have already suggested one way of proceeding, and it may be more feasible than a first glance would suggest. That is to say, it would probably work, but the feasibility of getting it adopted might seem low. Nevertheless, the probability of its working might offset the expected resistance to it. This plan is one that would require the passage of a rather simple law, or Supreme Court decision, and would require almost no administrative organization or police manpower to enforce. The law would state that any citizen who is an alcoholic or drug abuser, or one who at any given time is intoxicated from the effects of drugs or alcohol, cannot be held liable for debts. The constitutional basis for such a precedent would be the common-law doctrine that children cannot be held liable for debts, and the parallels between the immature child and the irresponsible drunk or drug abuser are readily apparent. Some of the consequences of such a law (assuming it would be honored in spirit as well as the letter) would include the following:

(1) Financial institutions would then require proof of non-alcoholism or non-drug-abuse before granting credit cards, mortgages, bank loans, or liability insurance. (2) The burden of proof, in order to establish non-liability for debt on the grounds of alcohol or drug abuse, would rest with the subject himself, rather than with the police or some other outside agency. (3) The subject thus denied opportunities for establishing credit will then be categorized as a lesser kind of American as measured by his capacity to handle responsibility, and, in addition, will be confronted by strong pressures that will serve to deter him from activities that would be dangerous to others.

Undoubtedly a great deal of progress can be made in raising the level of sophistication about the use of drugs and alcohol in the general public if a new campaign is kept to a reasonable level. For instance, it would be highly acceptable to the public to establish the following premises on which a campaign would be built: (1) That the use of drugs and/or alcohol is properly regarded by a great many citizens as a pleasurable experience that will not be denied them. By this very token, however, drinking or taking drugs should be properly confined to pleasurable, social occasions. The use of these substances clearly is not suitable or safe in certain other kinds of situations—namely, those in which one is confronted with major responsibilities, or when one is in control of potentially dangerous machines. Accordingly, the use of these substances at work, while driving an auto, flying a plane, or shooting a gun, is dangerous, even when the most responsible people are involved. Therefore, the aim of a progressive education campaign would be to eliminate the use of these substances, in any amounts, in those circumstances, but not at the expense of denying their use under safe social situations where pleasure and entertainment are the principal objectives. Again, as with the previously mentioned plan, this suggestion would highlight the relationship—and a very important one it is—between the use of drugs and alcohol, on the one hand, and the discharge of responsibility on the other.

TARGET POPULATIONS

A slogan-type campaign directed toward that portion of the population that is expected to be the most likely abusers of drugs and alcohol will be ineffective. This is the type of government or other publicly spirited program usually designed, and usually ineffectively for a youthful audience (e.g., campaigns designed to combat venereal disease, or the current advertising campaign against drugs). Unfortunately, the kind of audience, or target population, that these campaigns are meant for is not the one in communication with or responsive to the media or methods used. Instead, different kinds of programs must be designed for various kinds of populations that are, above all, in contact and responsive. Thus, cooperation should be elicited from practicing physicians to shift their practices and their education of patients to much less drug-oriented approaches, in order to start breaking down the prevailing belief in drug magic. Similarly, employers, and banks, insurance companies and other institutions should be involved in order to use the influence at their disposal. Not the least thing that all responsible citizens can do is to set better examples—and a reasonable one could well be an outgrowth of what was just discussed. That is, a new example by business and professional people, by police and judges, by teachers and salesmen, might be more effective than anything they might ever preach. The example in question would be the establishment in their own lives of a very clear, sharp, and unequivocal distinction between the times and places wherein drug and/or alcohol use is acceptable and those wherein it is not. Perhaps one of the most effective devices that could be used to discourage employees from using drugs and/or alcohol during working hours would be for the organization to fire a couple of executives for having a martini during a business lunch. There is an old tradition in medical circles that is followed rather closely, but is generally unknown to the public, so it does not serve a model-setting function. This tradition states that, when a new drug is introduced on the market, a physician should, "Prescribe it freely for your patients, rarely for your family, never for yourself."

In other words, an effective campaign needs to examine what groups in the population are in positions to exert an influence over the drug-taking and drinking behavior of other people, and concentrate on enlisting their cooperation—if necessary, granting them new powers to give or withhold privileges at their disposal (e.g., credit). Also, new campaigns need to focus attention on which groups in the population are in communication with the media available—and one of the unfortunate facts of life is that many of the less mature, more vulnerable groups are those with few ties to established modes of communication.

SPONSORING AND FINANCING
PREVENTIVE PROGRAMS

A most important factor that will determine the success or failure of a comprehensive, long-range preventive program will be the nature of the organization to which the responsibility is assigned, and the adequacy and stability of its financial resources. Clearly, the organization in question must be one that possesses the capability

NATIONAL COMMISSION ON MARIHUANA AND DRUG ABUSE: RECOMMENDATIONS

1. Eliminate penalties for possession or casual distribution.
2. Continue seizures of marihuana, continue its contraband classification, but cease arrests for possessing or transferring possession in lots of 1 ounce and less.
3. Public use, in contrast to private use, should be punished with moderate fines ($100).
4. Misdemeanors associated with marihuana use should be penalized with moderate fines of $100 or brief (60 days) jail sentences.
5. Driving autos while under the influence of the drug should be more severely dealt with, such as 1-year sentences or $1,000 fines.

The Commission announced the results of its investigation as indicating a need to reduce the severity of punishment as provided under existing laws. The danger of the drug has been over-emphasized, the Commission reports, and prosecuting users has been ineffective in bringing about control. Nevertheless, the Commission does not regard the time as appropriate to legalize the sale of the drug. A distinction was drawn between "private" use versus "public" use, and curbs on "public" use only were recommended.

Author's summary of recommendations made in the First Report of the National Commission on Marihuana and Drug Abuse, March, 1972, U.S. Government Printing Office.

of doing the job required and has or can acquire the degree of public acceptance and respect that would guarantee that its message would be heeded. There does not exist, now, any organization that would meet these requirements, although one or two might come close to fitting them.

From today's perspective, it seems highly unlikely that either a government agency or a private, profit-making organization is likely to command the widespread respect that would be necessary to insure an optimum chance for success, even if the technical expertise needed were present. Both these types of organizations are very likely to be suspect by some of the important groups in the population that have to be reached. A clearly non-business, non-profit type of organization that is not under direct government control would be most likely to fulfill these initial requirements. Organizations that now exist and that have these characteristics would include: The American Red Cross, The National Research Council, and The National Safety Council. Perhaps only recently organized groups, or at least organizations that have only recently come into public view, might acquire the kind of reputation mentioned; examples might include The Urban Coalition and the Sierra Club. In each case, in addition to public respect, some degree of expertise and a background of success has already been accumulated by these organizations in the

THE DRUG ABUSE OFFICE AND TREATMENT ACT OF 1972 (PL 92–255)

The preamble to the Act summarized "Congressional Findings" emanating from hearings and investigations:

1. Drug abuse is rapidly increasing.
2. Drug abuse seriously impairs the health of individuals and the well-being of society.
3. Drug abuse contributes substantially to crime.

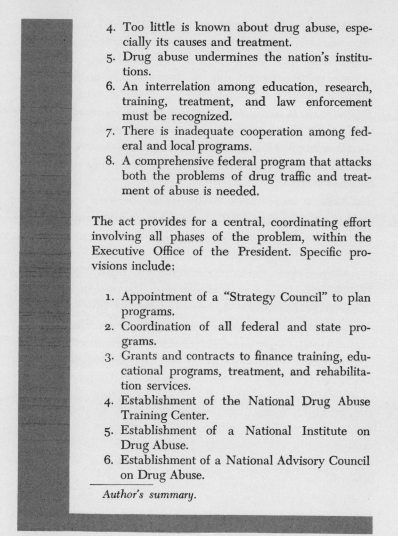

4. Too little is known about drug abuse, especially its causes and treatment.
5. Drug abuse undermines the nation's institutions.
6. An interrelation among education, research, training, treatment, and law enforcement must be recognized.
7. There is inadequate cooperation among federal and local programs.
8. A comprehensive federal program that attacks both the problems of drug traffic and treatment of abuse is needed.

The act provides for a central, coordinating effort involving all phases of the problem, within the Executive Office of the President. Specific provisions include:

1. Appointment of a "Strategy Council" to plan programs.
2. Coordination of all federal and state programs.
3. Grants and contracts to finance training, educational programs, treatment, and rehabilitation services.
4. Establishment of the National Drug Abuse Training Center.
5. Establishment of a National Institute on Drug Abuse.
6. Establishment of a National Advisory Council on Drug Abuse.

Author's summary.

area of public education. These kinds of organizations might be considered as candidates, then, to take on the task at hand. Actually, a kind of federation of these or-

ganizations might organize a supra-organization to under-
take the responsibility, or an entirely new organization
might be formed. If the second course is pursued, it would
require substantial periods of time for a new agency to
develop the kind of public reputation needed to have the
desired impact.

The financing sources for a long-range public education
program would be drawn from tax revenues collected from
the sale of all legal drugs and alcoholic beverages. As
mentioned before, it would make sense to categorically
designate a certain percentage of the revenues collected
by the federal government for the proposed preventive
program. A financing plan under which resources dwindle
or grow as consumption and the problem itself dwindles
or grows would be highly appropriate, and likely to meet
with public acceptance. A portion of the total budget thus
set aside in a categorical trust fund for the purpose would
also be devoted to research studies. Initially, the research
effort would be relatively large and the public education
effort relatively small, but as the latter was expanded, the
former would be curtailed.

Another logical choice for finding financial sources for
the program would be the imposition of a new federal
tax on all public advertising for drugs and alcohol. This
source would not appear to be particularly different from
a tax on the manufactured products, since it would ordinarily be assumed that such taxes would be passed on
to the consumer, as would be other taxes. However, in the
case of liquor, beer, and drug marketing—in contrast to
other consumer products—the profit margins and the percentage of gross sales spent on advertising are so large
(10 percent) that these taxes could easily be absorbed before being passed on to the consumer and would also serve
as an incentive to reduce the amount of advertising.

Furthermore, if the taxes increased to the point that all advertising was economically unfeasible, all but a few businessmen would benefit from its abolition. The public might also appreciate the poetic justice involved if the very efforts made by manufacturers to encourage drug and liquor consumption were being taxed to finance a program to discourage this consumption. Thus, if vested commercial interests sought to defeat the public education program, they could help bring this about by abandoning all their advertising, thus cutting off the program's funds, but meanwhile making the program less necessary.

There is a growing list of other industries in our country that are likely to be taxed in order to pay for the social cost of their doing business. Thus, automobile manufacturers are likely to be taxed in order to finance the task of disposing of junked automobiles, container companies will be taxed to pay for the cost of disposing of empty cans and bottles, and industries that contribute to pollution of air and water are likely to be taxed to pay for the social cost of eliminating pollution. In this context, then, it is appropriate also that those now legitimately making profits from drug and alcohol sales be taxed to pay for the social cost of the problems that arise from their abuse.

APPENDIX

SUGGESTIONS FOR SUPPLEMENTARY READING

GOVERNMENT PUBLICATIONS:

Drug Dependence, a periodical published by the National Institute of Mental Health (National Clearinghouse for Mental Heatlh Information), Chevy Chase, Maryland. Was changed to an abstract service in 1972.

Proceedings of the White House Conference on Narcotic and Drug Abuse, U.S. Government Printing Office, Washington, D.C., 1962.

Marihuana: a Signal of Misunderstanding, first report of the National Commission on Marihuana and Drug Abuse, U.S. Government Printing Office, Washington, D.C., 1972.

Second Interim Report by the Task Force on Prescription Drugs, Department of Health, Education and Welfare, Washington, D.C., 1968 (a study of Medicare drug costs and usage).

Hearings before the Subcommittee on Reorganization and International Organizations (88th Congress), *Interagency Coordination in Drug Research and Regulation,* U.S. Government Printing Office, Washington, D.C., 1963.

What You Should Know about the Alcohol and Tobacco Tax Division (Internal Revenue Service), U.S. Treasury Department, Washington, D.C., 1965.

Light Reading on News Events and American
Culture During the 1920–1940 Era
> *Only Yesterday: An Informal History of the 1920's,*
Frederick Lewis Allen, Perennial Library, 1931.
> *The Lawless Decade: A Pictorial History of a
Great American Transition,* Paul Sann, Bonanza Books, 1942.
> *The Desperate Years: A Pictorial History of the
1930's,* James Horan, Bonanza Books, 1962.
> *Since Yesterday,* Frederick Lewis Allen, Harper,
1940.
> *The Great Depression,* David Shannon, Prentice-
Hall, 1960.

Legislation, Law Enforcement, Crime, and Delinquency
> *The Legislation of Morality,* Troy Duster, The
Free Press, 1970.
> *Organized Crime in America,* Gus Tyler (editor),
Ann Arbor Paperbacks, University of Michigan Press, 1967.
> *The Opium Problem,* Charles Terry and Mildred
Pellens, New York Bureau of Hygiene, 1928.
> *Crimes Without Victims,* Edwin Schur, Prentice-
Hall, 1965.
> *The Addict and the Law,* Alfred Lindesmith,
Indiana University Press, 1965.
> *Delinquency, Crime and Social Process,* Donald
Cressey and David Ward (editors), Harper & Row, 1969.
> *Outsiders: Studies in the Sociology of Deviance,*
Howard S. Becker, The Free Press, 1964.

Drugs, Alcohol, and Social Issues
> *Marihuana Reconsidered,* Lester Grinspoon, Har-
vard University Press, 1971.
> *Drugs, Society and Human Behavior,* Oakley S.
Ray, C. V. Mosby Co., 1972.
> *The Drinking Man,* David McClelland, William
Davis, Rudolf Kalin and Eric Wanner, The Free Press, 1972.
> *Marijuana, the New Prohibition,* J. Kaplan, World
Publishing Co., 1970.
> *The College Drug Scene,* J. T. Carey, Prentice-Hall,
1968.

The Drug Experience, D. Ebin (editor), Grove Press, 1961.

Drugs: Medical, Psychological and Social Facts, P. Laurie, Penguin, 1967.

Narcotic Addiction, J. A. O'Donnell and J. C. Ball (editors), Harper and Row, 1966.

The Drug Users: The Psychopharmacology of Turning On, A. E. W. Smith, Harold Shaw Publishers, 1969.

The Drug Experience, D. Ebin (editor), Grove Press, 1961.

Society and Drugs: Social and Cultural Observations, R. H. Blum, Jossey-Bass, 1969.

The College Drug Scene, J. T. Carey, Prentice-Hall, 1968.

The Pharmaceutical Industry, W. Davies, Pergamon Press, 1967.

The Making of a Counter-Culture, T. Rosayk, Anchor Books, 1969.